White-Collar Crime

White-Collar Crime

John E. Ferguson Jr.

SERIES EDITOR
Alan Marzilli, M.A., J.D.

CHELSEA HOUSE
PUBLISHERS
An imprint of Infobase Publishing

White-Collar Crime

Chelsea House
An imprint of Infobase Publishing
132 West 31st Street
New York, NY 10001

Library of Congress Cataloging-in-Publication Data

Ferguson, John E.
 White-collar crime / by John E. Ferguson Jr.
 p. cm. — (Point/counterpoint)
 Includes bibliographical references and index.
 ISBN 978-1-60413-504-6 (hardcover : acid-free paper) 1. White collar crimes—
United States. I. Title. II. Series.
 KF9350.F47 2010
 345.73'0268—dc22
                                   2009032731

Chelsea House books are available at special discounts when purchased in bulk quantities for businesses, associations, institutions, or sales promotions. Please call our Special Sales Department in New York at (212) 967-8800 or (800) 322-8755.

You can find Chelsea House on the World Wide Web at http://www.chelseahouse.com.

Text design by Keith Trego
Cover design by Alicia Post
Composition by EJB Publishing Services
Cover printed by Bang Printing, Brainerd, MN
Book printed and bound by Bang Printing, Brainerd, MN
Date printed: June 2010
Printed in the United States of America

10 9 8 7 6 5 4 3 2 1

This book is printed on acid-free paper.

All links and Web addresses were checked and verified to be correct at the time of publication. Because of the dynamic nature of the Web, some addresses and links may have changed since publication and may no longer be valid.

Alan Marzilli, M.A., J.D.
Birmingham, Alabama

The POINT/COUNTERPOINT series offers the reader a greater understanding of some of the most controversial issues in contemporary American society—issues such as capital punishment, immigration, gay rights, and gun control. We have looked for the most contemporary issues and have included topics—such as the controversies surrounding "blogging"—that we could not have imagined when the series began.

In each volume, the author has selected an issue of particular importance and set out some of the key arguments on both sides of the issue. Why study both sides of the debate? Maybe you have yet to make up your mind on an issue, and the arguments presented in the book will help you to form an opinion. More likely, however, you will already have an opinion on many of the issues covered by the series. There is always the chance that you will change your opinion after reading the arguments for the other side. But even if you are firmly committed to an issue—for example, school prayer or animal rights—reading both sides of the argument will help you to become a more effective advocate for your cause. By gaining an understanding of opposing arguments, you can develop answers to those arguments.

Perhaps more importantly, listening to the other side sometimes helps you see your opponent's arguments in a more human way. For example, Sister Helen Prejean, one of the nation's most visible opponents of capital punishment, has been deeply affected by her interactions with the families of murder victims. By seeing the families' grief and pain, she understands much better why people support the death penalty, and she is able to carry out her advocacy with a greater sensitivity to the needs and beliefs of death penalty supporters.

The books in the series include numerous features that help the reader to gain a greater understanding of the issues. Real-life examples illustrate the human side of the issues. Each chapter also includes excerpts from relevant laws, court cases, and other material, which provide a better foundation for understanding the arguments. The volumes contain citations to relevant sources of law and information, and an appendix guides the reader through the basics of legal research, both on the Internet and in the library. Today, through free Web sites, it is easy to access legal documents, and these books might give you ideas for your own research.

Studying the issues covered by the POINT/COUNTERPOINT series is more than an academic activity. The issues described in the books affect all of us as citizens. They are the issues that today's leaders debate and tomorrow's leaders will decide. While all of the issues covered in the POINT/COUNTERPOINT series are controversial today, and will remain so for the foreseeable future, it is entirely possible that the reader might one day play a central role in resolving the debate. Today it might seem that some debates—such as capital punishment and abortion—will never be resolved.

However, our nation's history is full of debates that seemed as though they never would be resolved, and many of the issues are now well settled—at least on the surface. In the nineteenth century, abolitionists met with widespread resistance to their efforts to end slavery. Ultimately, the controversy threatened the union, leading to the Civil War between the northern and southern states. Today, while a public debate over the merits of slavery would be unthinkable, racism persists in many aspects of society.

Similarly, today nobody questions women's right to vote. Yet at the beginning of the twentieth century, suffragists fought public battles for women's voting rights, and it was not until the passage of the Nineteenth Amendment in 1920 that the legal right of women to vote was established nationwide.

What makes an issue controversial? Often, controversies arise when most people agree that there is a problem but disagree about the best way to solve it. There is little argument that poverty is a major problem in the United States, especially in inner cities and rural areas. Yet, people disagree vehemently about the best way to address the problem. To some, the answer is social programs, such as welfare, food stamps, and public housing. However, many argue that such subsidies encourage dependence on government benefits while unfairly penalizing those who work and pay taxes, and that the real solution is to require people to support themselves.

American society is in a constant state of change, and sometimes modern practices clash with what many consider to be "traditional values," which are often rooted in conservative political views or religious beliefs. Many blame high crime rates, and problems such as poverty, illiteracy, and drug use on the breakdown of the traditional family structure of a married mother and father raising their children. Since the "sexual revolution" of the 1960s and 1970s, sparked in part by the widespread availability of the birth control pill, marriage rates have declined, and the number of children born outside of marriage has increased. The sexual revolution led to controversies over birth control, sex education, and other issues, most prominently abortion. Similarly, the gay rights movement has been challenged as a threat to traditional values. While many gay men and lesbians want to have the same right to marry and raise families as heterosexuals, many politicians and others have challenged gay marriage and adoption as a threat to American society.

Sometimes, new technology raises issues that we have never faced before, and society disagrees about the best solution. Are people free to swap music online, or does this violate the copyright laws that protect songwriters and musicians' ownership of the music that they create? Should scientists use "genetic engineering" to create new crops that are resistant to disease and pests and produce more food, or is it too risky to use a laboratory to create plants that nature never intended? Modern medicine has continued to increase the average lifespan—which is now 77 years, up from under 50 years at the beginning of the twentieth century—but many people are now choosing to die in comfort rather than living with painful ailments in their later years. For doctors, this presents an ethical dilemma: should they allow their patients to die? Should they assist patients in ending their own lives painlessly?

Perhaps the most controversial issues are those that implicate a Constitutional right. The Bill of Rights—the first 10 Amendments to the U.S. Constitution—spells out some of the most fundamental rights that distinguish our democracy from other nations with fewer freedoms. However, the sparsely worded document is open to interpretation, with each side saying that the Constitution is on their side. The Bill of Rights was meant to protect individual liberties; however, the needs of some individuals clash with society's needs. Thus, the Constitution often serves as a battleground between individuals and government officials seeking to protect society in some way. The First Amendment's guarantee of "freedom of speech" leads to some very difficult questions. Some forms of expression—such as burning an American flag—lead to public outrage, but are protected by the First Amendment. Other types of expression that most people find objectionable—such as child pornography—are not protected by the Constitution. The question is not only where to draw the line, but whether drawing lines around constitutional rights threatens our liberty.

The Bill of Rights raises many other questions about individual rights and societal "good." Is a prayer before a high school football game an "establishment of religion" prohibited by the First Amendment? Does the Second Amendment's promise of "the right to bear arms" include concealed handguns? Does stopping and frisking someone standing on a known drug corner constitute "unreasonable search and seizure" in violation of the Fourth Amendment? Although the U.S. Supreme Court has the ultimate authority in interpreting the U.S. Constitution, its answers do not always satisfy the public. When a group of nine people—sometimes by a five-to-four vote—makes a decision that affects hundreds of millions of others, public outcry can be expected. For example, the Supreme Court's 1973 ruling in *Roe v. Wade* that abortion is protected by the Constitution did little to quell the debate over abortion.

Whatever the root of the controversy, the books in the POINT/ COUNTERPOINT series seek to explain to the reader the origins of the debate, the current state of the law, and the arguments on either side of the debate. Our hope in creating this series is that readers will be better informed about the issues facing not only our politicians, but all of our nation's citizens, and become more actively involved in resolving these debates, as voters, concerned citizens, journalists, or maybe even elected officials.

This volume looks at a category of crimes collectively known as "white-collar crime," referring to the fact that these crimes are often committed by seemingly respectable professionals such as accountants or bankers. Locks and burglar alarms can be used to protect our possessions, but people and businesses often see their entire savings wiped out by investment advisers who lie about what they are doing with their clients' money or companies that misrepresent their earnings in order to take advantage of investors. Although white-collar crime typically does not involve violence, it can often ruin people's lives.

The public needs to be protected from scandals such as those involving convicted Wall Street scammer Bernard Madoff or the corrupt and failed energy and communications firm Enron. However, sometimes overzealous prosecutors go after legitimate businesspeople, which some critics say has a chilling effect on business innovations. Further, there is considerable debate over the punishment handed out to white-collar criminals.

White-Collar Crime in the United States

"One of the greatest scoundrels, thieves, liars, criminals."[1] These are the words used by Nobel Peace Prize winner and Nazi concentration camp survivor Elie Wiesel. The target of these harsh words? Not a war criminal from World War II or even a current genocidal tyrant. Instead, these words were leveled against Bernard Madoff, a 70-year-old New Yorker who operated an investment firm. The action that sparked such intense vitriol from Wiesel was not a crime against humanity. It was not a murder. It was not even a simple assault. Instead, Madoff perpetrated a Ponzi scheme (a fraudulent investment operation) that defrauded thousands of investors of approximately $50 billion.[2]

In simple terms, Madoff took money from investors, telling them that he was investing it and reporting that they were getting big returns on their money. But he never invested the money. Instead, money from new investors was used to pay off

In this courtroom rendering by artist Christine Cornell, former Wall Street financier Bernard Madoff is led out of court in handcuffs. On March 12, 2009, Madoff pleaded guilty to a $50 billion Ponzi scheme in a federal court in New York City.

old investors. The problem with this scheme, as with all Ponzi schemes, is that eventually the newest investors need to be paid, and there are not enough first-time investors to cover the bills. After committing one of the biggest investment frauds in history, Madoff is serving a 150-year prison term.[3]

Yet the story does not end with the crime itself but endures in the lives of the investors. The Elie Wiesel Foundation for Humanity, one of Madoff's investors, lost all of its endowment. Because of the loss, the foundation was not able to open a center for Ethiopian refugee children in Jerusalem. Wiesel himself lost all of his life savings. Other investors included film director

Steven Spielberg, DreamWorks Animation chief executive Jeffrey Katzenberg, and Yeshiva University. Even international banks like Swiss giant UBS and the Royal Bank of Scotland were affected.[4]

The repercussions of this fraud rippled through American society. Two investors who lost their life savings committed suicide. Other individuals could no longer pay their rent or mortgages and were forced from their homes. Several foundations had to curtail their programs and offerings, or rebuild from almost nothing.[5]

What caused one man to do this much damage? How can society protect itself from this kind of massive harm committed by those who are well connected and have intellectual savvy? The notoriety surrounding Madoff's crimes and many other highly visible corporate frauds have led to increased interest in the area known as white-collar crime.

An Overview of White-Collar Crime

The concept of white-collar crime is relatively new. The term was first coined by an academic named Edwin H. Sutherland in a speech to the American Sociological Society's annual meeting on December 27, 1939. Sutherland explained that sociologists and economists had been missing something by not working with one another. In keeping their disciplines separate, they were ignoring a whole area of criminal activity that he dubbed "white-collar crime."[6] Sutherland used the term *white-collar* to differentiate crimes committed by professionals and those in the upper echelons of society (who typically wore white shirts with their business suits) from common or "street crimes" such as robbery, murder, or assault. It was also to highlight that these newly identified white-collar crimes did not involve violence or threats of violence but were often identifiable by their basis on fraud, trust, and craft.

Because Sutherland was one of the most popular criminologists of his time when he described this previously unstudied area of social deviance, people took notice. Newspapers covering the event described Sutherland's speech in detail and began to focus on the idea of white-collar crime. Before long, this concept took hold in the imagination of a public still stinging from the economic troubles of the Great Depression.

Even notorious criminals like Al Capone latched on to the concept of white-collar crime and bemoaned the seeming double standard in criminal conduct. Capone, who made a fortune selling liquor illegally during Prohibition, was quoted as saying: "Why don't they go after all these bankers who took advantage of thousands of poor people . . . in [Depression-era] bank failures? Isn't it a lot worse to take the last few dollars some small family has saved than to sell them a little beer, a little alky?"[7]

Defining White-Collar Crime

In order to understand white-collar crime, it is important to first understand the definition of crime itself. Sociologists say that "[a] crime is held to be an offense which goes beyond the personal and into the public sphere, breaking prohibitory rules or laws, to which legitimate punishments or sanctions are attached, and which requires the intervention of a public authority (the state or a local body)."[8] Sociologists, psychologists, and criminologists often look to these kinds of definitions as they focus not only on the rules and laws that are involved but also on the idea of deviance that underlies these theories. Lawyers, police officers, and others in the criminal justice system, however, are less concerned with the psychology behind these condemned actions and focus almost exclusively on the acts themselves and the laws that prohibit such acts. That is why *Black's Law Dictionary* defines crime as "[a] positive or negative act in violation of penal law; an offense against the State or United States."[9] To truly understand what this means, however, one must first look at how crime is treated in practice in the American judicial system.

Typically, any harm or wrong that is prohibited by a statute and committed against society as a whole is regulated by the criminal justice system. This idea stems from the ancient

Saxon concept of "breaching the King's peace"—crimes considered harmful to the king were therefore against all society. Even today, when a crime is committed against an individual, such as when one person murders another, the action is considered to be an offense against all of society. That is why when someone is charged with a crime, he or she is charged by the government and not the direct victim of the crime. If convicted, a criminal may be punished with monetary fines or confinement in jail. In some instances, the punishment may be the death penalty.[10]

The criminal justice system is far different from the civil justice system. Civil cases occur between individual parties and are often a result of a contractual dispute or other controversy that can be solved through a court restricting or requiring certain actions, usually a monetary payment. As opposed to criminal law, civil disputes do not result in jail time.

Although the differences between these two areas of law appear simple, the consequences of each are far more important. Once a law makes an action criminal, that action suddenly has a negative connotation. When someone is convicted of a criminal act, the conviction follows the person for life. In many instances this affects a person's ability to find employment, limits where he or she may live, and restricts the places he or she may travel or visit. In some instances it restricts a person's right to vote or own a firearm and places limits on other constitutionally protected rights. The protections related to criminal prosecution found in the U.S. Constitution are a result of the disadvantages associated with being convicted and labeled as a criminal.

If theorists (sociologists, social scientists, etc.) and practitioners (police officers, judges, lawyers, etc.) have clear working definitions of crime, then there would seem to be little trouble in defining white-collar crime within the umbrella already provided. In recent years, the term has become ubiquitous in everyday discussion and in the media. Universities and law schools have courses that focus entirely on white-collar crime. Yet both theorists and practitioners in the criminal justice system do not have an agreed-upon definition of white-collar crime.[11]

The problem with defining white-collar crime is where to draw the line between what is legal and what is illegal. Because most white-collar crime is connected to legitimate business activity, it is part of a continuum between legal business endeavors and illegal business practices. The father of white-collar crime, Edwin H. Sutherland, defined the term as a "crime committed by a person of respectability and high social status in the course of his occupation."[12] People quickly came to see the weaknesses in such a definition, since it does not detail what acts should be considered crimes.

The legal code is particularly sparse in describing white-collar crime, with few references outside a specific area that deals primarily with accounting practices.[13] The Federal Bureau of Investigation (FBI) has an entire division dedicated to white-collar crimes, which it defines as crimes

> categorized by deceit, concealment, or violation of trust and are not dependent on the application or threat of physical force or violence. Such acts are committed by individuals and organizations to obtain money, property, or services, to avoid the payment or loss of money or services, or to secure a personal or business advantage.[14]

This rather broad definition includes such crimes as "money laundering, securities and commodities fraud, bank fraud and embezzlement, environmental crimes, fraud against the government, health-care fraud, election law violations, copyright violations, and telemarketing fraud."[15] This evolution from Sutherland's rather simple definition to the expansive working definition that law enforcement uses today is one of the areas of controversy that will be dealt with in later chapters.

White-Collar Crime in History

Throughout history, defrauding or cheating people has been considered immoral and wrong, even in the absence of specific legal prohibitions. Religious moral codes have long provided prohibitions against fraud. Jews and Christians know that the Ten Commandments require them not to steal or bear false witness, while Muslims note that the Koran clearly states, "O you who believe, wherefore do you say what you do not? Very hateful is it to God, that you say what you do not."[16]

In the Western legal tradition, attempts at avoiding fraud and other forms of theft through trickery led to many laws aimed at curbing such behaviors. Usually these laws were created after a problem had occurred, that is once people had been cheated or deprived of their property in some way that society found noxious. One noteworthy example of this impulse occurred in the early 1930s. In the aftermath of the Great Depression, legislators sought to regulate or criminalize many business activities that had been legal, yet had led to one of the greatest collapses of financial markets the world had seen. Sutherland's speech itself was in response to the effects of the Great Depression and the actions that had allowed the economic collapse to occur.[17]

Since that time, legislators have continued to struggle over what should be criminalized and what should be protected. In a free-market society, all transactions involve some form of risk. How to manage that risk so that innocent people are not harmed while still allowing for the free working of the markets has been a constant struggle. While theorists look to the harm actions cause, practitioners look to what can equitably be regulated, and in some cases, criminalized. As stated earlier, all of these struggles are made more difficult because of the effect of being labeled a criminal can have on a person. New technology only expands the difficulty of these problems because people can now conduct business electronically. This convenience exponentially increases both the benefits and the dangers of business and the ability of some to abuse the system for ill-gotten gains.[18]

Currently, white-collar crime is prosecuted under a variety of laws, including those meant to combat mail fraud, embezzlement, theft, organized crime, corporate malfeasance, and

Excerpts from the National Check Fraud Center: Types and Schemes of White-Collar Crime

Bank fraud: To engage in an act or pattern of activity where the purpose is to defraud a bank of funds.

Blackmail: A demand for money or other consideration under threat to do bodily harm, to injure property, to accuse of a crime, or to expose secrets.

Bribery: When money, goods, services, information or anything else of value is offered with intent to influence the actions, opinions, or decisions of the taker. You may be charged with bribery whether you offer the bribe or accept it.

Computer fraud: Where computer hackers steal information sources contained on computers such as: bank information, credit cards, and proprietary information.

Counterfeiting: Occurs when someone copies or imitates an item without having been authorized to do so and passes the copy off for the genuine or original item. Counterfeiting is most often associated with money; however, [it] can also be associated with designer clothing, handbags, and watches.

Credit card fraud: The unauthorized use of a credit card to obtain goods of value.

Currency schemes: The practice of speculating on the future value of currencies.

Embezzlement: When a person who has been entrusted with money or property appropriates it for his or her own use and benefit.

Environmental schemes: The overbilling and fraudulent practices exercised by corporations [that] purport to clean up the environment.

unsafe products and medicines. Regulatory agencies such as the Securities and Exchange Commission (SEC) also monitor and enforce regulations against corporations for such actions

Forgery: When a person passes a false or worthless instrument such as a check or counterfeit security with the intent to defraud or injure the recipient.

Health care fraud: Where an unlicensed health care provider provides services under the guise of being licensed and obtains monetary benefit for the service.

Insider trading: When a person uses inside, confidential, or advance information to trade in shares of publicly held corporations.

Insurance fraud: To engage in an act or pattern of activity wherein one obtains proceeds from an insurance company through deception.

Investment schemes: Where an unsuspecting victim is contacted by the actor, who promises to provide a large return on a small investment.

Kickback: Occurs when a person who sells an item pays back a portion of the purchase price to the buyer.

Money laundering: The investment or transfer of money from racketeering, drug transactions or other embezzlement schemes so that it appears that its original source either cannot be traced or is legitimate.

Racketeering: The operation of an illegal business for personal profit.

Securities fraud: The act of artificially inflating the price of stocks by brokers so that buyers can purchase a stock on the rise.

Tax evasion: When a person commits fraud in filing or paying taxes.

Telemarketing fraud: Actors . . . place telephone calls to residences and corporations [and request] a donation to an alleged charitable organization, or where the actor requests money . . . or a credit card number up front and does not use the donation for the stated purpose.

Source: "National Check Fraud Center: Types and Schemes of White-Collar Crime." http://www.ckfraud.org/whitecollar.html.

as trading irregularities, corporate malfeasance, and reporting irregularities. Nongovernmental licensing groups—such as the associations and boards that license attorneys, doctors, and other professionals—also monitor for white-collar crime and other deviant behavior. The wide range of laws and regulations used to prosecute white-collar crime further illustrates the broad nature of these crimes.[19]

Scamming by E-Mail

A scam that has become prevalent since the advent of e-mail is the so-called Nigerian fraud scam. This particular fraud changes in its specifics, but usually involves an e-mail sent from a supposed high-ranking official from an African nation. The author of the e-mail wants the recipient to open a shared bank account and deposit a few hundred to a few thousand dollars into the account. The e-mail author explains that the money will be used to cover transaction fees so that the "official" can deposit millions of dollars into the shared account in an effort to get the money out of the country. Once the money is out of the country, they can split it between them. Obviously no money is ever deposited from the scammer, but this fraud continues to make the rounds. Below is a sample e-mail (with misspellings included):

Date: Fri, 3 Jun 2005 08:58:18 -0700 (PDT)
From: Moses Odiaka [mosesadiaha@go.com]
To: XXXXXXXX
Subject: CONFIDENTIAL PROPOSAL

My name is Mr. Moses Odiaka. I work in the credit and accounts department of Union Bank of NigeriaPlc, Lagos, Nigeria. I write you in respect of a foreign customer with a Domicilliary account. His name is Engineer Manfred Becker. He was among those who died in a plane crash here in Nigeria during the reign of late General Sani Abacha.

Since the demise of this our customer, Engineer Manfred Becker, who was an oil merchant/contractor, I have kept a close watch of the deposit records and accounts and since then nobody has come to claim the money in this a/c as next of kin to the late Engineer. He had only $18.5 million in

Legislating White-Collar Crimes

In the first years of the twenty-first century, several major corporations, including Enron Corporation, were struck by economic upheaval when it came to light that their accounting practices made them look as if they were far more profitable and better financed than they actually were. Many of these companies—once touted as among the safest places to invest

his a/c and the a/c is coded. It is only an insider that could produce the code or password of the deposit particulars. As it stands now, there is nobody in that position to produce the needed information other than my very self considering my position in the bank.

Based on the reason that nobody has come forward to claim the deposit as next of kin, I hereby ask for your co operation [sic] in using your name as the next of kin to the deceased to send these funds out to a foreign offshore bank a/c for mutual sharing between myself and you. At this point I am the only one with the information because I have removed the deposit file from the safe. By so doing, what is required is to send an aplication [sic] laying claims of the deposit on your name as next of kin to the late Engineer. I will need your full name and address telephone/fax number, company or residential, also your bank name and account, where the money will be transfer [sic] into.

Finally i [sic] want you to understand that the request for a foreigner as the next of kin is occassioned by the fact that the customer was a foreigner and for that reason alone a local cannot represent as next of kin. When you contact me, then we shall discuss on how the money will be split between us and others we shall also speak in details. I am currently in europe [sic] for a six months course, you can reach me on this number for further discussion XXXXXXXXXXXX. Kindly send your reply to my private email address stated below.

Trusting to hear from you,
I remain Respectfully yours,
Mr Moses Odiaka.

Source: FraudGallery.com. http://potifos.com/fraud/2005-06-03.html.

money—crumbled, and the investors who believed in them were left without savings. Many retirees were required to return to the workforce, as their retirement accounts were decimated by the failures of these companies.[20]

In response, Congress passed the Sarbanes-Oxley Act in 2002, one of the first major U.S. laws to deal expressly with white-collar crimes. This law required more stringent accounting practices and more transparent financial dealings and imposed increased jail sentences for anyone convicted of white-collar crimes. What would have seemed unthinkable a few years earlier was being put into practice by 2003. Corporations were put on notice.[21]

Despite such legislation, white-collar crime remains troublesome in a number of ways. One of the greatest problems is that white-collar crime is hard to define. What exactly is acceptable business practice, and what is criminal activity? While it is easy to identify harms to society, it is much harder to actually regulate the conduct that may lead to those wrongs, especially if one is trying to maintain as much personal and economic freedom as possible.

The second area of controversy has to do with how convicted white-collar criminals are penalized. People often complain that white-collar criminals are sentenced to prisons that resemble resorts instead of corrections institutions. Coupled with the low probability of getting caught, some argue that white-collar crime is not really discouraged at all. Others counter that white-collar crime only deals with money and should not be treated as harshly as violent offenses.

Finally, there is a great deal of debate over how much government regulation is needed or appropriate to deal with white-collar crime. The banking and financial market crisis that brought on the severe economic recession that began in late 2007 had led some to advocate for more government oversight of these areas. Others argued that more oversight leads to less efficient markets and less freedom.

Summary

White-collar crime is an increasingly important issue in American society. As a type of criminal activity, it is hard to define, thus making it difficult to appropriately address through the current means of criminal-justice practice. While not a new area of social deviance, white-collar crime has been the subject of new laws and government regulation in recent years. Problems facing this issue include clearly defining white-collar crime, dispensing appropriate penalties, and providing the appropriate level of government oversight and regulation.

Too Many Activities Are Considered White-Collar Crimes

O n any given day, employees of GlaxoSmithKline, a drug company, conduct business in predictable, mundane ways. Administrative assistants will answer phones. Mail will be sorted in mailrooms. Managers will call meetings. And thousands of pages of documents will be shredded. This shredding will take place for a number of reasons: to protect the privacy and security of clients, to comply with laws requiring destruction of certain items, to remove old files and make way for new ones, and even just to clean off desks. Most employees will engage in this activity with little or no thought. But after events in 2001 and 2002, people who work in some offices have had to rethink how they shred. For some office workers, improper shredding could result in 20 years in prison.

How could such a common practice result in a prison sentence? In the wake of the implosion of the Enron Corporation and the economic fallout it caused, Congress passed a law commonly referred to as the Sarbanes-Oxley Act. This law specifically includes a section that creates criminal penalties of up to 20 years in prison if a person, in certain circumstances, shreds or otherwise alters documents needed for litigation.[1] This has caused companies across the nation to scramble to create "document retention policies" that will meet the new standards required by Sarbanes-Oxley, as well as provide legal protection for the company and employees. Making this process all the more complicated are the myriad federal laws and regulations that require businesses to destroy documents that may endanger the privacy rights of clients. Adding to the complexity, e-mails and voice mails have also been included in many of these laws, so retention policies must be crafted not only for paper documents but also for electronic communications.[2]

For many companies, dedicating hours of employee time and other resources to creating and implementing document retention policies is just the beginning. There are hundreds, if not thousands, of laws that require companies to spend time and money on activities that have nothing to do with their primary business. The law of unintended consequences controls the result of all this legislation. What was meant to disrupt those attempting to perpetrate fraud on an unsuspecting public has become so onerous that innocent businesses and their employees are at risk of unintentionally engaging in now-criminalized activities. Ultimately this leads to a climate of fear in American business that stifles creativity and risk-taking.

Even those who do not violate any laws are saddled with enormous compliance costs. In 2009, the Competitive Enterprise Institute reported that 2008 compliance costs for U.S. businesses hit $1.172 *trillion.* These kinds of additional costs could prompt companies to relocate to countries with less regulation or cause some to shut down completely.[3]

Some regulation is, of course, needed. Yet the desire by some to make every potentially bad action a crime has numerous consequences. The reality is that not every bad business decision is a crime. Sometimes, such decisions are just acts of poor judgment or risks that do not work as expected. For society, fueled by politicians and the media, to create criminals out of businesspeople whose job it is to take risks hurts American and global economies. Finally, the attempt to criminalize certain types of business activity is actually far more a function of social bias and social engineering than a way to keep people safe from harm. Simply, much that is called white-collar crime is not a matter of criminal activity but a matter of class bias.

Not every bad act is a crime.

People may not like many things in daily life, whether it is sitting next to someone who smells bad or paying for a movie that turns out not to be worth the price of admission. Although these kinds of nuisances are annoying and can deprive a person of some enjoyment or money, they certainly do not rise to the level of criminal conduct. No one would seriously suggest that those who do not bathe frequently enough or the directors of bad movies deserve to be put in jail or classified as criminals. Encountering these unpleasant situations is simply the risk of daily life in a free society.

In much the same way, people assume a certain level of risk when they enter into the business world. No investment is truly risk proof, nor should it be. The premise of capitalism as practiced in the United States is that those who willingly risk money on a business venture have the opportunity to either gain or lose, but the choice is theirs. Taking away the possibility of losing also means taking away the possibility of succeeding. Although the risk of capitalism has brought about some abuses—as in the Enron and Madoff scandals—it has also led to far more success stories, as exemplified by Bill Gates, Steve Jobs, and Warren Buffett. Calculated risk has made the U.S. economy the single most important economic force in the world.[4]

Even if one wanted to change the U.S. economic system to reduce the risk of harm or loss, the criminal justice system is a poor tool for achieving this result. In the United States, the criminal justice system is designed to stop people from intentionally causing harm to society. This may mean stopping one person from beating up another (which leads to fear of violence in the broader society) or stopping one person from lying and stealing from another (which leads to less trust in economic transactions). Because the effects of these actions are so damaging to society, the consequences can include loss of liberty (prison) or even loss of life (death penalty). Clearly the criminal justice system is designed to stop the greatest harms to society. It is not meant to micromanage people's business decisions.

This does not mean that people who are violated in business have no recourse. The U.S. legal system also has a civil component that allows people who are wronged to file suit against those who have harmed them. If the lawsuit is successful, the party that is harmed is usually provided with monetary compensation. This is the best approach in dealing with most business problems.

Perpetuating the notion that certain business practices are crimes when they are really administrative or civil issues unjustly creates pariahs. If a person is convicted as a felon, he or she loses many rights. Beyond losing his or her freedom by being placed in prison, the criminal also loses the right to vote, the right to associate with others, even the right to privacy as government oversight continues during probation. This is a disproportionate and unfair penalty for engaging in business practices that some find unpleasant.

Criminalizing business activities hurts the economy far more than it protects individuals.

Most laws that are designed to stop white-collar crime are drafted with the best of intentions. When an interviewer asked Senator Paul Sarbanes about the Sarbanes-Oxley Act, he explained:

A number of very major, highly regarded public companies, along with their auditors, were relying upon convoluted and often fraudulent accounting devices to inflate earnings, hide losses, and drive up stock prices.... The purpose of the Sarbanes-Oxley Act goes beyond addressing recent scandals to building a durable framework on the foundation laid by the Securities Acts of 1933 and 1934. We have set standards for honest, transparent, and ethical business practices in our great public companies and established the safety mechanisms to keep them in place.[5]

A Timeline of Securities Regulations

Since its inception, the United States has had a vibrant financial system that has enabled individuals to invest money in companies, thus gaining some level of ownership in that company. When the company makes profits, those who invested get a share of those profits. These ownership investments are often referred to as stocks and are bought and sold through stock brokerages and on stock exchanges, such as the New York Stock Exchange (NYSE) or the National Association of Securities Dealers Automated Quotations (NASDAQ). To make profitable investments, investors need valid and accurate information about companies. Following the 1929 stock market crash on Wall Street and the Great Depression that followed, Congress passed many bills to regulate investments and keep investors better informed, avoid fraud, and stabilize markets.

1933—Securities Act

This act regulated how corporations could issue securities, required investors to be given prospectuses, and mandated filing requirements before securities could be made available.

1933—Banking Act

This act, also known as the Glass-Steagall Act, abolished the practice of banks acting as brokerage firms. It also established the Federal Deposit Insurance Corporation to protect customers' bank deposits.

elements of a company's activities. In some cases, audits were required in sections of a company's financial statements that were so inconsequential that they involved only one-five hundredths of one percent of a firm's net income. Some reported cases have included auditors investigating and reporting which employees have keys to buildings and the numbers of letters in employees' passwords.[6]

A company's purpose is to make money, not perform needless yet expensive audits. If a company has to perform additional measures, the cost of these requirements will be passed on to consumers. Some regulations are necessary to ensure consumers are safe and have the information they need. But too many regulations can drive up costs and harm the ability of companies to perform efficiently. The balance between efficiency and safety/information is a delicate one.

Criminalizing business and intellectual activity is not only expensive, it also skews the business decision process. When companies create plans and models for doing business, they can calculate the administrative or civil fines they may be liable for, depending on the risk of their business. But criminal sanctions are hard to calculate because they may result not only in monetary fines but also in prison.

Broadening criminal laws to encompass risky or innovative business decisions should not be allowed or else entrepreneurs will stop taking risks, thus hurting the economy and lessening America's standing in the business world. As John Berlau of the Competitive Enterprise Institute explains in an article, "Freedom and Its Digital Discontents," risk will always be managed. It is part of every business. The question is: Should the government or the markets manage it? Berlau, and many like him, clearly believe that the innovative capabilities of the market are far better at managing and controlling risk than government oversight.[7]

Senator Sarbanes and others who drafted and voted for this bill clearly intended to help American investors by making the financial situation of companies more transparent. Unfortunately, this bill included sections that criminalized what had previously been non-criminal business decisions. It also included hefty requirements for auditing and disclosure. Although ensuring that more information is provided to investors and stakeholders might sound like a good idea, Sarbanes-Oxley also created hundreds of millions of dollars in compliance costs for companies. Many of these requirements involved complicated and expensive auditing of minor

1934—Securities Exchange Act

In response to President Franklin D. Roosevelt's urging that Congress do more to regulate the markets, Congress created the Securities and Exchange Commission with this act. This agency was given power to oversee security exchanges and impose rules and fines on those who manipulated the markets.

1970—Securities Investor Protection Act

Funded by fees charged to brokers, this insurance fund was designed to protect investors in the event their brokerage firm went bankrupt.

1984—Insider Trading Sanctions Act

This law imposed penalties of up to three times the ill-gotten profits for those convicted of insider trading.

1999—Gramm-Leach-Bliley Act

This controversial law repealed the Glass-Steagall Act and allowed banks to operate as security brokerages as well.

2002—Sarbanes-Oxley Act

This law created a host of new regulations and oversight provisions designed to ensure greater transparency and standardization in corporate accounting.

Source: "SEC Historical Society: Virtual Museum and Archive of the History of Financial Regulation." http://www.sechistorical.org/museum/timeline/index.php.

A number of very major, highly regarded public companies, along with their auditors, were relying upon convoluted and often fraudulent accounting devices to inflate earnings, hide losses, and drive up stock prices. . . . The purpose of the Sarbanes-Oxley Act goes beyond addressing recent scandals to building a durable framework on the foundation laid by the Securities Acts of 1933 and 1934. We have set standards for honest, transparent, and ethical business practices in our great public companies and established the safety mechanisms to keep them in place.[5]

A Timeline of Securities Regulations

Since its inception, the United States has had a vibrant financial system that has enabled individuals to invest money in companies, thus gaining some level of ownership in that company. When the company makes profits, those who invested get a share of those profits. These ownership investments are often referred to as stocks and are bought and sold through stock brokerages and on stock exchanges, such as the New York Stock Exchange (NYSE) or the National Association of Securities Dealers Automated Quotations (NASDAQ). To make profitable investments, investors need valid and accurate information about companies. Following the 1929 stock market crash on Wall Street and the Great Depression that followed, Congress passed many bills to regulate investments and keep investors better informed, avoid fraud, and stabilize markets.

1933—Securities Act

This act regulated how corporations could issue securities, required investors to be given prospectuses, and mandated filing requirements before securities could be made available.

1933—Banking Act

This act, also known as the Glass-Steagall Act, abolished the practice of banks acting as brokerage firms. It also established the Federal Deposit Insurance Corporation to protect customers' bank deposits.

Even if one wanted to change the U.S. economic system to reduce the risk of harm or loss, the criminal justice system is a poor tool for achieving this result. In the United States, the criminal justice system is designed to stop people from intentionally causing harm to society. This may mean stopping one person from beating up another (which leads to fear of violence in the broader society) or stopping one person from lying and stealing from another (which leads to less trust in economic transactions). Because the effects of these actions are so damaging to society, the consequences can include loss of liberty (prison) or even loss of life (death penalty). Clearly the criminal justice system is designed to stop the greatest harms to society. It is not meant to micromanage people's business decisions.

This does not mean that people who are violated in business have no recourse. The U.S. legal system also has a civil component that allows people who are wronged to file suit against those who have harmed them. If the lawsuit is successful, the party that is harmed is usually provided with monetary compensation. This is the best approach in dealing with most business problems.

Perpetuating the notion that certain business practices are crimes when they are really administrative or civil issues unjustly creates pariahs. If a person is convicted as a felon, he or she loses many rights. Beyond losing his or her freedom by being placed in prison, the criminal also loses the right to vote, the right to associate with others, even the right to privacy as government oversight continues during probation. This is a disproportionate and unfair penalty for engaging in business practices that some find unpleasant.

Criminalizing business activities hurts the economy far more than it protects individuals.

Most laws that are designed to stop white-collar crime are drafted with the best of intentions. When an interviewer asked Senator Paul Sarbanes about the Sarbanes-Oxley Act, he explained:

Attempts to broaden laws against white-collar crime are acts of class bias, not sound criminal justice.

If excessive regulation costs more than its benefits and if most business decisions are outside the competencies of the criminal justice system, then why is there such a drive for more white-collar-crime regulation? Why the popular cry for more laws and criminalization of business practices? The answer may lie in the origins of white-collar crime theory itself.

John Baker of the Heritage Foundation believes that Professor Edwin H. Sutherland specifically meant to capitalize on the class warfare brewing at the time he made his famous speech. Baker describes how Sutherland was unconcerned about traditional theories of criminal justice involving intent and pre-sumptions of innocence:

> Sutherland goes on to construct a class-based definition of "white-collar crime." He is concerned with who the alleged perpetrator was, rather than what that person might have done. "White collar crime," says Sutherland, is "crime committed by a person of respectability and high social status in the course of his occupation." With this radical redefinition, Sutherland attempted to drain the word "crime" of its meaning. He made distinctions not on the basis of an act or intent, but according to the status of the accused.[8]

The problem with Sutherland's approach is that it focuses not on the actions or even the harm caused by the actions in question, but on *who* perpetrated the actions. This kind of approach is counter to the U.S. justice system and the Constitution on which it is founded. Under the Constitution, laws must be applied equally to all people. The Constitution does not allow, for example, one set of laws for white Americans and another set of laws for black Americans. Nor does it allow the law to apply differently for either rich or poor.[9]

Despite the legal prohibition against treating people of different socioeconomic statuses differently, Baker argues that Sutherland was intent on creating a class-based conflict. There was populist support for this kind of attack on the rich due to the ongoing harm many felt from the Great Depression. Targeting the rich was an easy political gambit, and it retains its currency to this day, as evidenced by the general disdain and animosity being heaped on the rich in the wake of more recent financial scandals.[10]

The danger of this kind of class warfare, however, is that it can cause irreparable damage to society when taken to the extreme. If all risk taking is prohibited, professionals will move to places where they are able to be creative and take risks. If the rich and professionals were to leave the country, they would take

Differences Between Criminal and Civil Law

	Criminal	Civil
Parties	Society (State) v. the individual	Individual v. individual
Case names	*United States v. Smith*	*Smith v. Marx*
Penalties	Jail time, monetary penalties, loss of some rights	Monetary damages
Purpose	Protect society from dangerous elements, rehabilitate those who do wrong, punish those who break laws, prevent future harms to society	Make parties whole after failure or harm caused by one party or the other.

with them not only their physical assets, but also their experience, skills, intelligence, and training. This kind of brain drain would be disastrous for any nation, but especially so for the United States, which has long been acknowledged as being on the cutting edge of innovation.

Summary

When an investment fails, or a business goes under, those who put money into these ventures want to place blame for their loss. Yet criminalizing risk taking does not really help anyone. In fact, it ultimately harms all people in society by dampening the entrepreneurial spirit at the core of the American economy. It also has the unintended side effect of diluting the meaning and power of the criminal justice system, thus making it less effective in keeping people safe from real crimes.

Despite the desire of those who lose out, and the political opportunists who use the pain of these so-called victims to inflate their own positions, not every bad thing that happens to a person is necessarily criminal. Often these are just the risks associated with living and doing business in a free society. Shortsighted attempts at regulating and removing these risks do little to help those who have lost and eventually lead to all members of society losing out because risk-reducing strategies typically harm the larger economy. Ultimately, the desire to broaden the classification of white-collar crime to other business activities is really a matter of class warfare, based more on bias and perception than any sense of objective wrongs or criminal activity. Criminalizing the actions of the rich and the professional classes will only cause them to leave this country, taking with them their talents, resources, and skills.

More Activities Should Be Classified as White-Collar Crimes

Few people enjoy filing their taxes, but 12-year-old Gabriel Jimenez seemingly wanted to file several times. In the mid-1990s, his mother received notices from the Internal Revenue Service (IRS) that her son, who worked as a child model, had filed more than one return. After investigating, Gabriel's mother found that her son's Social Security number had been stolen by someone who was using it to set up an alternate life, complete with loans, multiple accounts, and credit cards. Twelve years later, Gabriel was still plagued by problems resulting from his identity theft, from having his power turned off in the middle of winter (due to several overdue accounts on homes he had never lived in) to not being able to qualify for student aid because of his questionable credit report.[1]

Bronti Kelly did not even get to pay his taxes. He could not get a job. After his wallet was stolen several years earlier, the thief used his information when arrested for burglary, arson, and shoplifting. Because the police reports were filed under Kelly's name, he was turned down from hundreds of jobs for which he was otherwise qualified. Never given any explanation for why he was not hired, he eventually tracked down an information clearinghouse used by employers that listed him as a security risk because of "his" criminal record. Even after clearing the matter with the police, submitting his fingerprints on file, and receiving a "Certificate of Clearance," Kelly was not able to find employment. Out of options, he filed for bankruptcy, lost his apartment, and lived out of his car. When things still did not improve, Kelly was forced to live in parking garages to stay out of the elements and bathed in his former apartment complex's pool.[2]

Yet these accounts seem almost minor when compared with the tragic ending of two professionals in the late 2000s. In December 2008, 65-year-old hedge-fund manager Thierry de la Villehuchet was found dead in his New York office with cuts on his wrists, forearms, and upper arms. Six months later, in June 2009, on a park bench in Southampton, England, a highly decorated soldier and United Nations aid worker, William Foxton, was found with a self-inflicted gunshot wound to the head. While separated by an ocean and several months, these sad situations were connected, as both men had lost large sums of their own and other people's money in the Ponzi scheme operated by Bernard Madoff. Unable to cope with the aftermath, they took their own lives.[3]

What do a retired soldier, a hedge-fund manager, a retail sales associate, and a 12-year-old boy all have in common? They were all victims of white-collar crime. For these four people, and the millions of victims of white-collar crime like them, the effects of these crimes can be as debilitating and devastating as any physical attack. Often this is because a physical or traditional criminal attack occurs only once, while some white-collar crimes haunt a person for decades.[4]

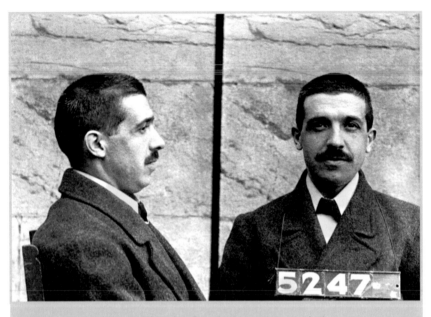

These mug shots show Charles Ponzi, the early twentieth-century embezzler for whom Ponzi schemes are named.

Unfortunately, white-collar crimes are not pursued with the same vigor as more visible street crimes. Because of their complex nature, white-collar crimes are often not considered as serious as street crimes. Also, the victims are frequently blamed for their involvement in the activity that led to the crime. Thus, despite the economic and physical harms that white-collar crime causes, it fails to receive the necessary attention or focus it deserves.[5]

Such thinking, however, is shortsighted. Because of their professional nature, white-collar crimes also tend to have effects that reach far beyond the immediate criminal incidence. These ripple effects touch the lives of thousands upon thousands of people, in both large and small ways, often for years. Though usually not highlighted, the ramifications of white-collar crimes often go beyond the financial, affecting people physically, mentally, and emotionally.[6]

White-collar crimes are often not taken seriously.

Throughout U.S. legal history, white-collar crimes have never received the same kind of attention and policing focus as street crimes. While many factors influence the level of policing focus, four carry the lion's share of responsibility: the difficulty law enforcement has in investigating and prosecuting white-collar crime, the tendency to blame the victim, sporadic political will, and infrequent reporting by victims.[7]

The experience of Gabriel Jimenez's mother in trying to stop the person who stole her son's Social Security number is an example of this first difficulty. When initial attempts to get the police to help were unsuccessful, she tracked down the identity thief on her own. When she again sought law enforcement assistance and tried to pass on the information and location of the criminal, the police still said they could not help her.[8] Why would law enforcement fail to help a victim, even turning down valuable information and evidence?

The biggest problem most law enforcement officials have in dealing with white-collar crimes is the complexity of the crimes, which often involve financial and legal transactions that fall into gray areas of the law. These crimes also tend to require far more resources to investigate and prosecute, including the use of consultants and experts who can decipher the frequently complex relationships involved.[9]

In Gabriel's case, there was also the problem of jurisdiction. When Social Security numbers are involved, the matter is usually dealt with by federal agencies, especially the IRS. At the same time, simple fraud cases usually fall within the jurisdiction of local law enforcement. This led to inaction by both federal and local law enforcement in Gabriel's situation.[10]

Another barrier to more rigorous attention to white-collar crimes is shared with cases of rape. In both rape and white-collar crime, there is a tendency by the public and the victims themselves to have a "blame the victim" mentality. The mechanisms for perpetrating white-collar crimes, especially ones like fraud, are one reason people are quick to blame the victim. Since the victims voluntarily give the fraudsters their money, trusting them to invest or otherwise appropriately use the money, the victims are seen as being somehow complicit. This is in sharp

Excerpt from the National Check Fraud Center: Types of White-Collar Schemes

Advanced fee schemes: Actor induces victim to give him some type of advanced fee in return for a future benefit. The future benefit never occurs, and [the] victim never receives the advanced fee back.

Check kiting: A bank account is opened with good funds and a rapport is developed with the bank. Actor then deposits a series of bad checks but prior to their discovery, withdraws funds from the bank.

Coupon redemption: Grocery stores amass large amounts of coupons and redeem them to manufacturers when, in fact, merchandise was never sold.

Directory advertising: Actor either impersonates [a] salesperson from a directory company like the Yellow Pages or fraudulently sells advertising [that] the victim never receives.

Home improvement: Actor approaches a home owner with a very low estimate for a repair or improvement. Inferior or incomplete work is performed. Once the repairs are completed, actor intimidates the victim to pay a price much greater than the original estimate.

Inferior equipment: Actors travel around selling inferior equipment, such as tools, at high prices.

Land fraud: Actor induces victim to purchase [tracts] of land in some type of retirement development [that] does not exist.

Odometer fraud: Unscrupulous used-car salesman purchases used cars and turns back the odometers. The used car is sold at a higher price due to its low mileage.

Pigeon Drop: Actor No. 1 befriends the victim. Actor No. 2 shows both Actor No. 1 and victim a "found" package containing a large amount of cash. Actor No.

contrast to traditional street robbery, when the robber forcibly takes valuables from the victim.[11]

The view that victims of fraud and similar white-collar crimes are "getting what they deserve" is not limited to just the

---

1 insists that the found money be divided equally but only after each person puts up his own money to demonstrate good faith. All the money is put in one package and the package is later switched.

Police impersonation: Actor tells victim that his bank is being operated by fraudulent bank officers. Actor instructs victim to take money out of [the] bank and place it into a good bank. After the money is withdrawn, the actor allegedly takes the money to the police station for safe keeping. The victim never sees the money again.

Ponzi: An investment scheme where the actor solicits investors in a business venture, promising extremely high financial returns or dividends in a very short period of time. The actor never invests the money [but] does pay dividends. The dividends consist of the newest investors' funds. The first investors, pleased to receive dividends, encourage new investors to invest. This scheme falls apart when the actor no longer has sufficient new investors to distribute dividends to the old investors or the actor simply takes all the funds and leaves the area.

Pyramid: An investment fraud in which an individual is offered a distributorship or franchise to market a particular product. The promoter of the pyramid [says] that, although marketing of the product will result in profits, larger profits will be earned by the sale of franchises. For example, if a franchise price is $10,000, the seller receives $3,500 for every franchise sold. Each new franchise purchaser is presented with the same proposal so that each franchise owner is attempting to sell franchises. Once the supply of potential investors is exhausted, the pyramid collapses. Many times, there are no products involved in the franchise, simply just the exchange of money.

Source: "National Check Fraud Center: Types and Schemes of White-Collar Crime." http://www.ckfraud.org/whitecollar.html.

victims and the public. Even the criminals often see the victims as greedy and somehow at fault for being involved in the scam. Often, they rely on the victims' desire to make a fast buck as the basis for the fraud. In other instances, such as when a company fails to provide the safety equipment needed for employees, the desire to blame the victim still persists. The employer alleges that the employee was negligent or reckless. But, as in rape cases, the problem with having a victim-blaming mentality is that it skews the attention from what should be the focus of policy makers—stopping the criminal activity.[12]

The problem of blaming the victim leads to the other two major barriers to better enforcement of white-collar crimes— namely, sporadic political efforts to strengthen laws against white-collar crimes and the failure of victims to report these crimes. While politicians frequently scramble to pass new legislation when a high-profile problem gains national attention, as seen in the Bernard Madoff case, most of the time legislators give this area of the penal code little attention. Realizing that the public does not see white-collar crimes as high a priority as street crimes, politicians take little action.[13]

Even reporting the crimes committed against a person can be a daunting task. Many victims do not report white-collar crimes because they are too embarrassed at being tricked. They do not want to be judged as victims by the police officers taking their reports. Making matters worse, victims seldom receive even a fraction of their lost assets back. Between feeling like "second-class citizens" in the criminal justice system and the minimal likelihood of any return, it is little wonder that most people do not report white-collar crimes.[14] The underreporting of white-collar crimes leads some to argue that they are not as problematic for society as others believe. This creates even less incentive for politicians to invest political capital into passing harsher laws, and the victims receive even less protection.

White-collar crimes often spread far beyond the immediate victim.

Given the response from authorities and policy makers, it would seem that street crime is far more damaging to society than white-collar crime. Yet that is clearly not the case. Several studies have found that, when compared with street crime, white-collar crime has a far greater reach, both in terms of how long the effects last as well as how many others are affected. Research done on people who had lost everything in the savings and loan crisis of the 1980s and 1990s, when hundreds of financial institutions failed, found that the effects of this event lasted for years. Depression and stress-related health problems are common. One study found that, within two years of one white-collar criminal incident, 29 percent of the victims suffered a major bout of depression. For some, financial ruin had further health effects, as they were no longer able to afford health care or the expensive medications some were required to take.[15]

And the spiral of harm goes beyond the immediate victims of the crime. Once all financial resources were depleted, many people were left to default on obligations such as mortgages, debts, and other bills. This results in harm to everyone who did business with the victims. Such economic effects are seen in the victims of the Madoff scam; charities that had invested with Madoff were no longer able to help those who depended on them.

More than 50 years ago, Edwin Sutherland foresaw the dangers to the fabric of society caused by white-collar crime: "Because it violates trust, white-collar crime breeds distrust, lowers social morale, and 'attacks the fundamental principles of American institutions.'"[16] Those who have been victimized by white-collar criminals frequently lose faith in the government and its ability to protect citizens. Such lack of trust and faith can eventually lead to people disengaging from public life altogether.

Summary

White-collar crimes are a clear danger to society. The failure of authorities to institute policies that more strongly protect against white-collar crimes is a failure to understand the crimes and the damages they inflict. Lack of understanding, under-reporting, and victim blaming may lead to some of these deficiencies, but the harms are great enough that white-collar crime must be taken seriously by the criminal justice system.

White-Collar Penalties Are Too Lenient

I n 1982, the small town of Hohenwald, Tennessee, was shaken to its roots. One of the two banks in town was the victim of a fraud by a criminal who passed several large checks. These bad checks eventually caused the bank to become insolvent, or unable to pay its debts, and the federal government had to take it over. The con man was arrested and tried, but the money was gone. Everyone in Hohenwald felt the ripple effects of this crime, but no one more than Carol Halbrooks.

The regulators now running the bank required Halbrooks, the owner of a small business in town, to repay her short-term business loans immediately. She also lost her credit line, and eventually, her business. The stress of the situation led to the death of her husband. Soon after, she lost their home. Having sold all her possessions to pay the bills, she was left with nothing but her car, which she lived in. Reduced to rummaging through trash bins for food and collecting cans for change, this once proud small-business owner, taxpayer, and wife found herself foraging on the fringes of American society.

The ray of hope that eventually saved Halbrooks turned out to be Columbia State Community College in Columbia, Tennessee. Through loan programs at the school, Halbrooks was able to start to work on a new life. It was not easy. She was a 41-year-old widow who lived in her car. She studied by the streetlights while parked in scary parts of town. But she was determined to make it.

Then one day, something unexpected happened. As she sat in an auditorium, waiting for her next class, she looked up and saw John Candler Jr., the con artist who had defrauded the bank and sent Halbrooks on her downward spiral. As part of a prison program, Candler was there to warn students of the consequences of criminal activity. In an effort to scare students away from a life of crime, he told of the hardship of cold showers and how irritating the prison laundry's detergent was. He said how he could not wait for his release in a few months, so that he could get back to his own bed and be with his family.

This was too much for Halbrooks. Unable to listen anymore, she stood up and screamed:

> I don't have a home to go to, thanks to you! . . . You got it made! You get food three times a day and you have a bed to sleep on! You should have to live on the streets and try to make your own way with nothing! You should have people look away from you so that they will not have to acknowledge your existence![1]

Embarrassed at her own outburst, Halbrooks rushed from the auditorium, but not before hearing the applause of students and faculty alike, most of whom had not known of her history or situation.[2]

Kenneth Lay, the former Enron chairman, and his wife, Linda, leave court during the thirteenth week of his fraud and conspiracy trial in 2006. Lay was found guilty on May 25 of 10 counts against him and faced 20 to 30 years in prison. Before his scheduled October 23 sentencing, he died on July 5, 2006, while vacationing.

White-collar crimes cause great damage to individuals and society.

Sadly, Halbrooks's situation is not an isolated one. Although white-collar crimes are not as damaging as street crimes like murder and rape, they can cause devastation that spreads far beyond the immediate victim. In Halbrooks's case, the harm to the bank resulted in the government having to take it over, which in turn caused the bank to call in her business loans. In this way, secondary victims like Halbrooks, who had never had any dealings with Candler, end up losing everything. And then there are victims who were hurt by Halbrooks's inability to pay her debts. This ripple effect shows that economic damages can spread far beyond what either the criminals or the victims can imagine.[3]

(continues on page 48)

Famous White-Collar Criminals and Their Crimes

Jérôme Kerviel (charged in 2008, trial pending in 2010)

A former trader at the French bank Société Générale, Kerviel manipulated the bank's computer system to make the bank appear exceptionally profitable. This eventually led to nearly €5 billion ($7.4 billion) in losses. Interestingly, investigators could find no benefit to Kerviel other than the rush of beating his colleagues.

Bernard Madoff (convicted 2009)

The founder of Bernard L. Madoff Investment Securities, he lost $50 billion of investor money in blatant fraud. He took in billions of dollars and failed to invest any of it. His crime is thought to be the most expensive white-collar crime in history.

Walter Forbes (convicted 2007)

The former CEO of Cendant manipulated company books to make Cendant appear more profitable. Revelation of his actions led the market value of the firm to fall $14 billion in one day.

Kenneth Lay (convicted 2006)

The former CEO of Enron sold off millions of dollars in stock just before Enron went bankrupt. He was ultimately convicted of fraud and conspiracy but died of a heart attack before sentencing.

Jeffrey Skilling (convicted 2006)

Much like his Enron CEO predecessor, Kenneth Lay, Skilling sold millions in stock just before Enron went bankrupt. He was convicted of 19 counts of conspiracy, insider trading, securities fraud, and lying to auditors, and was sentenced to more than 24 years in prison.

Bernard J. Ebbers (convicted 2005)

The former CEO of WorldCom required $11 billion in expenses to be listed as profits. When it was revealed, WorldCom stock fell from $60 a share to mere pennies. He was sentenced to 25 years in prison.

L. Dennis Kozlowski (convicted 2005)

The former CEO of Tyco International was convicted of misappropriating $400 million of company money for personal use, including a $1 million birthday party for his wife that he claimed was a shareholder meeting.

John Rigas (convicted 2004)

The former CEO of Adelphia Communications Corporation stole $2.3 billion from the company for personal use.

Andrew Fastow (convicted 2004)

The former chief financial officer of Enron was convicted of wire and securities fraud. It was the special third-party companies that Fastow created that ultimately led to the loss of faith in Enron and resulted in the failure of the company.

Eddie Antar (convicted 1993)

The former owner of the Crazy Eddie chain of stores, Antar skimmed money from the business while inflating company profits in preparation of going public. When the company went bankrupt, he had already sold his shares and made a huge profit. He was convicted on 17 counts of fraud.

Michael Milken (convicted 1990)

Nicknamed the "Junk Bond King," Milken was indicted on 98 counts of racketeering and tax evasion. He pled guilty to six securities and reporting violations. Sentenced to 10 years, he served less than two.

Ivan Boesky (convicted 1986)

Boesky made $200 million in illegal trades on Wall Street, was fined $100 million, and spent two years in prison. He once claimed, "I think greed is healthy."

Stanley Goldblum (convicted 1973)

As the president of Equity Funding, he falsified insurance policies and scammed insurance companies. When the fraud was revealed, his company's investors lost $300 million.

Ivar Kreuger (committed suicide in 1932 before he could be arrested)

Known as "The Match King," Kreuger was one of the richest men in the world, making loans to nations like Spain, Poland, and Romania. Ultimately his financial adventures in the United States led him to make fraudulent statements about certain investments to bolster investor confidence. When the truth came out, his fortunes unraveled.

Charles Ponzi (convicted multiple time from the 1910s to the 1930s)

One of the best-known fraudsters, Ponzi is credited with creating the so-called Ponzi scheme, which requires getting a steady flow of new investors and using

(continues)

(continued)

their money to pay out earlier investors. Ponzi's original scheme was based on purchasing stamp coupons for immigrants through foreign exchange markets.

Cassie Chadwick (convicted 1905)

Born Elizabeth Bigley, Chadwick was convicted of fraudulent banking loans and forging Andrew Carnegie's signature to a security note backing her loans. Her lifetime of fraud and aliases ultimately led to prison, where she died in 1907.

Sources: http://www.blackvoices.com/work-money/top-financial-villains-biggest-white-collar-criminals; http://www.biography.com/notorious/crimefiles.do?action=all&catId=266319; http://www.nytimes.com/1993/07/21/business/crazy-eddie-founder-guilty-of-fraud.html.

(continued from page 45)

    The public does not often realize the damage white-collar crime causes because the costs are so hard to identify and measure. Direct costs—such as the amount embezzled in a fraud—are relatively easy to calculate, but quantifying the cost of, for example, an unsafe work environment is harder. In many financial crimes, the costs are spread over many victims, making the damages harder to detect. Also, many white-collar crimes occur in the business world in which large corporations are the victims. Most people find it difficult to empathize with these victims and therefore are not interested in the crimes.[4]

    What most people do not realize is that white-collar crimes are far more economically damaging than any street crime. Some estimate that white-collar crime causes $1 trillion in economic losses each year in the United States—10 to 50 times greater than the annual cost of street crimes such as theft and robbery.[5] The victims in these cases, whether they are huge corporations or individuals, will have to make up those losses somewhere. Ultimately, everyone pays for white-collar crime, whether through higher taxes or higher prices for goods and services.[6]

Indirect costs of white-collar crime are just as massive. Enforcement agencies have to hire officers to investigate white-collar crimes. The courts have to use their limited resources to prosecute those who are caught, often in expensive trials that require pricy expert witnesses to explain the complicated crimes. Regulators require monitoring and reporting systems so that crimes are detectable, thus costing businesses and consumers even more. Then there are all of the costs associated with health and safety hazards that occur due to environmental, workplace, and health-care frauds; these costs are nearly impossible to quantify.[7]

Clearly, white-collar crimes are not victimless or just about money. These crimes affect the lives of people in innumerable ways. Surely the people who perpetrate such crimes are deserving of the harshest of punishments.

Penalties for white-collar crimes are too lenient.

While the victims of white-collar crimes, like Carol Halbrooks, are often left to their own devices, the perpetrators of such crimes often end up far better off. White-collar offenders, if they are ever caught and tried, are usually sent to minimum-security federal prison camps. Back in the 1980s, these prison camps were dubbed "Club Fed," a sarcastic reference to a popular vacation resort chain, because of the comparatively luxurious lifestyle prisoners were allowed. Before public outrage stopped the practice, prisoners at the Eglin facility in Florida were allowed to wear their own clothes, have food delivered from outside, and even go home in the evenings to have dinner with their families.[8] Other facilities around the country still have amenities such as fitness centers, music programs, organized team sports, and vocational training. The Morgantown facility in West Virginia is in the Blue Ridge Mountains, where prisoners wake to picturesque views and "the sight of deer grazing on the compound."[9] The Otisville facility in New York caters to Orthodox Jewish prisoners, offering a kosher kitchen and a rabbi on site, and flying prisoners to Seder meals.[10]

The comforts of such detention facilities are sadly disproportionate to the level of harm these criminals cause. Even though
minimum-security facilities have instituted new restrictions,
they still provide housing, clothing, three nutritious meals a day,
educational and vocational training, and recreation—making
these criminals better off than many of their victims, who are
often unable to afford basic necessities.

Far worse than the lenient conditions prisoners encounter
is the reality that most white-collar criminals do not even get
caught, and when they do, their sentences are lighter than those
who commit comparable street crimes. Ivan Boesky and Michael

White-Collar Criminals and the Amounts They Stole

	Scammer	Amount of fraud (adjusted for inflation)	Years served in prison
1	Bernard Madoff	$50 billion	Sentenced to 150 years on July 1, 2009
2	Jérôme Kerviel	$7.4 billion	Awaiting trial
3	Bernie Cornfeld (1970)	$2.3 billion	0.92
4	Michael Milken (1986)	$1.6 billion	2
5	Tino De Angelis (1963)	$1.2 billion	7
6	Stanley Goldblum (1973)	$1.2 billion	8
7	Ivan Boesky (1986)	$163 million	1.83
8	Barry Minkow (1989)	$151 million	5
9	Charles Ponzi (1920)	$ 17.9 million	5

Source: Brad Zigler, "The Felon Index," *Registered Rep*, October 1, 2002, http://
registeredrep.com/mag/finance_felon_index/.

Milken both spent less than two years apiece for their crimes. And incredibly, Milken was allowed to leave prison with $500 million of his ill-gotten gains.[11] Had these men committed street crimes such as bank robbery or theft in these amounts, they would have spent at least 5 to 12 years in prison.[12] And street criminals would not end up in a minimum security "camp," but in a real prison with hardened criminals, barbed wire, and watchtowers. If they had been sentenced for trafficking in a handful of crack cocaine, they would have had to serve 22 years.[13] Something is wrong when $30,000 worth of crack cocaine puts a person in prison for 22 years, while Boesky's and Milken's crimes merit less than a full two years of prison time.[14]

Inadequate punishment of white-collar criminals fails to curb criminal conduct.

The criminal justice system punishes criminals through deterrence, retribution, incapacitation, and rehabilitation. Deterrence means that the punishment should be severe enough that it would prevent a potential criminal from committing a similar crime. Retribution is the idea that criminals should get their "just reward" for their crimes and that society is avenged through the punishment of wrongdoers. Incapacitation is the hope that, by removing a criminal from society, society is saved from further crimes. Finally, rehabilitation is the desire to have the penal system reform criminals through vocational training and therapy, so they become productive members of society when released.[15]

Unfortunately, the punishment white-collar criminals face often falls far short of any of these goals. When white-collar criminals are allowed to serve their often-short sentences watching deer in the mountains while playing on the camp soccer team and taking violin lessons, they are not likely to be deterred from crimes that could make them millions or even billions of dollars. Neither the individual who is caught, nor others in a similar situation, are likely to be frightened away from crime based on these sentences.

As for retribution, one has only to look at some of the victim statements given to the judge in Bernard Madoff's trial. Burt Ross, a former mayor who lost $5 million in Madoff's scheme, told the judge, "Seven hundred years ago, the Italian poet Dante in *The Divine Comedy* recognized fraud as the worst of sins, the ultimate evil. . . . [Madoff should be punished] to the maximum allowed by law."[16] Another victim, Kathleen Bignell, explained to the judge, "I told my father (89) he could not die because we didn't have enough money to bury him. This is what we are reduced to after Madoff lived so well off of all of our money."[17] Finally, after describing Madoff as "a thief and a monster," Jesse Cohen told the judge, "Please make sure that the facility in which he rots is extremely uncomfortable."[18] The retribution sought by the victims who lost everything, and the society that witnessed the aftermath of the fraud on everyday people, would not likely be assuaged if Madoff lived out his last years at a cushy facility.

As for incapacitation and rehabilitation, neither is likely to happen when white-collar criminals are given such relatively short sentences. From 1991 to 2001, white-collar criminals were sentenced on average to 19 to 20.8 months. During that same time, drug offenders received average sentences of 71.7 to 88.2 months.[19] Because of the enormous impact of their crimes, white-collar criminals should be punished on the same level, if not more severely, than street criminals like drug dealers. This means lengthy sentences at real prisons, as well as making restitutions to all those who are harmed by the crime. David Feige wrote in *The Nation*:

> [T]hough extended confinement . . . may be something of a deterrent, relative rarity and palatable conditions of confinement severely limit the deterrent effect on those considering multimillion-dollar schemes that run afoul of the law. Put bluntly, it's not irrational to steal $10 million if the worst-case scenario is a few years in

Camp Fed. But change that sentence to read Sing Sing or Attica or Pelican Bay and what emerges is a whole new calculus of crime.[20]

Summary

Currently, white-collar criminals are not punished adequately in relation to the amount of harm they cause. White-collar crimes cause exponentially more economic damage than street crimes, yet street crimes garner far more attention. Unless they are high-profile cases stemming from large losses, white-collar crimes are seldom even prosecuted. If found guilty, a white-collar convict usually spends little time in jail, and the jail itself is almost always a minimum-security facility. Because of their leniency, the penalties for white-collar crime fail to meet the goals of the criminal justice system. In fact, they are so limited in severity that they make it almost irrational to follow the law.

White-Collar Penalties Are Appropriately Harsh

In late 2008 and early 2009, public outcry erupted in the wake of the revelations about the Ponzi scheme run by Bernard Madoff. On the news and across the Internet, people bemoaned the trust violated by Madoff and the effects of his actions.[1] Clearly Madoff harmed many people, and for that, he deserved to be punished. But what kind of punishment is fair and just?

Suggestions found everywhere from victim statements to Internet blogs indicated some pretty grim punishments for Madoff. Few claim to be satisfied with the idea of Madoff serving a typical jail term. Victim Robert G. Mick commented, "Mr. Madoff deserves no better than to live under a bridge in a cardboard box, scavenging for his food and clothing."[2] Cries for "the maximum sentence allowed" and "no mercy" were common.[3] Others seemed to think Madoff should consider his prison term as "a good time to reflect on suicide."[4] Some went as far as to argue that the United States should follow China's example and execute white-collar criminals.[5] Op-ed columnist Ron Shinkman even rationalized executing people like Madoff for the greater good: "If there's a candidate for a non-murderer to be executed for deterrent effect, Madoff is it.... There are a lot of people out there who aspire to be the next Madoff.... The chance they might be executed if they go too far might actually give them some pause."[6]

Many of those who clamor for harsher punishments, especially those directly affected by white-collar crime, are often exhibiting an emotional response to injustice. To some extent, they have a right to be upset, since they were harmed by a criminal action. But should the administration of justice be left to the emotions of a mob mentality?

The reality is, white-collar crimes are simply not the same as violent street crimes. And the differences between the two are clear. White-collar crimes tend to be economic crimes in which violence is not a factor. They are often committed while a professional is engaging in complex business situations that are fraught with opportunities to run, quite accidentally, afoul of the law. Finally, legislators, judges, and legal scholars carefully craft the punishments given to white-collar criminals so that they will meet the goals of the criminal justice system and be the most fair and just means for society to respond to this kind of deviant behavior.

White-collar crimes are economic crimes and should be treated accordingly.

When people look at Bernard Madoff or Michael Milken or even Charles Ponzi, they see primarily the fraud and the vast amounts of money that thousands of people lost. What they often forget is that, while these fraudsters committed criminal acts, they were not the only willing parties involved. Unlike a common street criminal, Madoff did not subdue his victims in a dark alley at gunpoint. Milken never murdered anyone to get her jewelry. Ponzi never pulled a gun inside a bank and demanded all the money. Instead, these men were able to commit their crimes because their victims wanted something from them. By voluntarily giving their money to these men, the victims hoped to get rich.

This is not to say that criminal acts did not occur. Clearly white-collar criminals actually do commit crimes. But the crimes they commit are usually not committed alone. Often others are needed, whether they are investors wanting to make big returns without having to work for them or office staff who turn a blind eye when environmental-safety standards are not "exactly" met. To put all of the responsibility on the criminal without taking into account the culpability of the victim or society releases people from having to be responsible for their own good and bad decisions. Especially in investment frauds, it is often clear when looking back that if something is too good to be true, it probably is—and investors should have some responsibility in checking into their own investments.[7]

While white-collar crime may cause economic harm and even damage the trust people have in one another, it still does not rise to the level of violent crime. To try to create comparable punishments for embezzlement and violent assault or rape or murder denigrates the seriousness of these latter crimes. Victims may lose money in a white-collar crime, but in a violent crime people lose their physical security, control over their bodies, and in some cases, even their lives.[8]

Despite claims to the contrary, white-collar offenders are getting ever-longer sentences. Criminal defense lawyer and adjunct law professor Harlan Protass is concerned with the way sentencing of white-collar criminals is handled. Since many of the high-profile, higher-dollar crimes are tried in federal courts, judges use federal sentencing guidelines, which employ a mathematical formula to calculate the punishment in relation to the severity of the crime. In white-collar cases, this calculus is based on the size of the financial harm. In some higher-profile cases, embezzlers or fraudsters would be punished more severely (and in some cases *far* more severely) for their nonviolent crimes than murderers or sex offenders.[9]

The trend in recent decades is toward ever-harsher penalties. While the white-collar criminals of the 1980s may have been given lighter sentences, since Enron's collapse in 2001, judges have not been so lenient. One need only look at the Madoff sentence—150 years for a senior citizen—to see how this trend is playing out in the courts.[10] Giving life sentences to elderly criminals seems disproportionate, especially when they committed no physical harm to anyone, while murderers, sex offenders, and arsonists receive far less time.

The penalties are far harsher when looked at comparatively.

Clearly, losing one's livelihood, personal fortune, standing in the community, and personal freedom are harsh realities for anyone. These punishments are far greater for those convicted in white-collar crimes, since they often live in the upper socioeconomic strata of society. A street criminal who is incarcerated for mugging someone to get money for another drug fix hardly loses out and arguably improves his or her lot in life through incarceration. While prison is no resort, it does provide the drug addict with three meals a day, a place to sleep indoors, and potential access to medical and addiction resources.

Compare such a sentence with that of a white-collar criminal like Martha Stewart. Her crime: conspiracy and obstructing justice over a $51,000 stock deal that no one seemed to be able to prove was illegal in the first place. Before sentencing, Stewart spent her time in one of her three homes, each elegant and impressive by any standard, and ran a multibillion-dollar business. After sentencing, she was stripped of her presidency at the company she had built from scratch, fined $250,000, and sentenced to five months in a women's prison. For her prison term, she was required to live in a dormitory with up to 150 other

Martha Stewart leaves federal court in New York City on July 16, 2004, after being sentenced to five months in prison for lying to investigators about a stock sale.

women. She slept on a bunk bed. Each two-woman section had only low walls separating it from the rest of the dorm, and there were no doors anywhere. Accentuating the loss of privacy and complete lack of control over her daily life, Stewart was immediately strip-searched upon her arrival.[11]

While it is often hard for many people to feel sorry for the rich and famous, looking objectively at the disparity in the two previous cases clearly shows a huge difference in what was lost. Punishment in the justice system must not be based on class biases and envy of those who have more. The rules and punishments must be fair and objective. It seems far harsher for someone like Martha Stewart to lose so much for doing so little, while violent criminals lose comparatively less for transgressions that damage society far more.

The sentences handed down reflect the goals of the penal system.

When judges hand down a punishment, it should meet at least one of four main goals: deterrence (keeping the criminal and others from trying this crime again), retribution (society wants revenge), incapacitation (removing the criminal from society), and rehabilitation (reforming the criminal to be a productive member of society upon release). As previously explained, the current system of punishment attempts to meet these goals through fairly harsh punishments. Despite these punishments, societal pressure to increase penalties for white-collar crimes threatens to skew the goals and effectiveness of the system.[12]

The penalties facing white-collar criminals prove to be an effective deterrent. The reality is that once convicted of white-collar crimes, these criminals are less likely to offend again than street criminals. Professor Ellen S. Podgor of Stetson University College of Law explains, "Because white-collar criminals forfeit their positions of power, experience regulatory restrictions, and suffer community shame, they are unlikely to be repeat offenders."[13]

Similarly, retribution is an easily understandable impulse but difficult to incorporate into a legal system in ways that remain fair while satisfying public desire. For instance, cases of industrial espionage hardly spur people onto the streets demanding the death penalty for the perpetrators. Yet at the Madoff sentencing, that is exactly what happened.[14] Should the emotions generated from having a sympathetic victim dictate how people are punished? Surely not. Compounding this situation is the real danger that treating white-collar crimes the same as violent street crimes trivializes the street-crime victim's violent experience.

An Interview with a Former Partner at Arthur Andersen, LLP

In writing this book, the author interviewed a former partner at Arthur Andersen, LLP, the accounting firm that was caught up in the Enron scandal. After retiring from Andersen, "Ms. Smith"—whose name cannot be revealed due to ongoing litigation—began to teach at a midsize college in Texas but remains involved in accounting through her service on many boards and agencies. This interview provides her perspective on what ultimately led to the demise of Enron and Andersen.

According to Ms. Smith, Enron was an aggressive trading company that was known for pushing the limits of business practices, a culture that led the company to take ever-greater risks. These aggressive practices resulted in incredibly complex organizational structures and complicated accounting situations.

Enron's complicated trading structure relied heavily on the trust of those who bought and sold energy in the energy markets. When this trust was eroded, Enron collapsed, several of its top executives were convicted of white-collar crimes, and even its accounting firm, Andersen, was convicted of impropriety based on aggressive accounting practices and suspicious-looking document shredding. When asked to explain more about the accounting issues, Smith remarked:

> Ignoring any fraud, there were two key accounting issues and one public perception problem in the Enron case. The first issue related to the company's use of "mark-to-market" accounting. While this was a valid principle under Generally Accepted Accounting Principles (GAAP), it required the company to estimate the fair value of long-term energy contracts. Enron was aggressive in their estimates. This made Enron particularly vulnerable to market changes.

This point is particularly important: Investors had to be able to trust Enron's estimates. When the energy markets shifted, Enron's estimates were seen as too aggressive for some, who lost faith in Enron's capabilities as energy traders. Smith continued:

> The second accounting issue related to their use of "special purpose entities" (SPEs). Publicly traded companies are rarely one entity. Instead, they

Incapacitation is also met by the current system of punishments. Part of sentencing of white-collar criminals often includes restrictions on future employment; for example, stock traders

are many entities consolidated or combined into one reporting company. SPEs are a special entity type, which, if they meet certain criteria, do not have to be consolidated with the reporting company. They are legitimately used by many companies for legitimate purposes. In Enron's case, some of the SPEs were apparently formed only to move assets and debts off the books and create a favorable financial picture. Additional loans would then be obtained and guaranteed by Enron stock. Some of the provisions had "triggers" based on Enron's stock price. If the stock price fell below certain trigger points, Enron would have to assume the debt. As a result, Enron's financial structure was particularly vulnerable to a decline in their stock price.

Enron's financial structure was complex. "Mark-to-market" and "SPEs" were legitimate accounting practices. However, their use to intentionally present a false financial picture is not.

These mini-companies, or SPEs, eventually led to many of the convictions in the Enron scandal. While it is acceptable to create mini-companies inside of a bigger company, for special business purposes, it is not acceptable to do so just to hide debts or make a company look more profitable than it is. Smith, however, believed Andersen's problems were of a different stripe:

Andersen started having problems over the headlines about shredding of documents. Despite all the headlines, shredding was not illegal. It is a normal part of any audit. People don't realize the sheer quantity of paper generated in an audit. You have to shred it because no one has enough room to store it all. The timing, however, raised suspicions.

While Andersen was eventually vindicated by the Supreme Court, the damage had been done. All of the bad press from the arrest of Enron executives and the misperceptions about Andersen's role caused a loss of trust. For both trading companies like Enron and public accounting firms like Andersen, trust is foundational for business. When the trust was gone, so was the business.

From Smith's perspective, criminal acts destroyed Enron. Public misunderstanding and bad press killed Andersen.

convicted of insider trading are no longer allowed to be stock traders. And even in cases in which the court does not impose such restrictions, professionals convicted of a white-collar crime are unlikely to be able to return to the industries in which they had worked. This limits the access and ability to the means of committing future white-collar crimes.[15]

QUOTABLE

William R. Mitchelson Jr. and Mark T. Calloway

In the *National Law Journal*, William R. Mitchelson Jr. and Mark T. Calloway describe one modern aspect of getting arrested—the "perp walk." The following is an excerpt:

Can the defendant avoid being handcuffed and arrested in full view of the media, which often are tipped off to the arrest, and then paraded about by the police while the cameras click and videos record? Unfortunately, for criminal defendants, the answer often is no.

Known as the "perp walk," this practice is becoming an increasingly common and popular media phenomenon. Once largely reserved for notoriously violent crimes that threatened the safety and security of the community, the perp walk has been extended to indicted chief executive officers and other corporate executives. . . .

Rudolph Giuliani is given credit for "patent[ing] the perp walk" for white-collar defendants during his tenure as U.S. attorney for the Southern District of New York. . . . When the time came to arrest three prominent Wall Street traders and bankers that his office accused of insider trading, Giuliani directed that the defendants be arrested at their offices, handcuffed and escorted from the building to a mob of press that had been previously alerted. Charges against one of the defendants were dismissed, although damage to his reputation based on the perp walk and media frenzy was irreparable. . . .

The courts have indicated that letting the public know that a criminal prosecution has commenced is a proper government function; imposing humiliation on the accused before a finding of guilt isn't.

Source: http://www.law.com/jsp/ihc/PubArticleIHC.jsp?id=1142862090121.

Finally, rehabilitation is not really met by more prison time. Doing dishes in the prison kitchen is not going to help the Michael Milkens of the world become productive members of society after being released. As Martha Stewart explained in a blog from prison, society would be better served if first-time offenders were part of rehabilitation programs. In prison, she

QUOTABLE

Harlan Protass

Criminal defense attorney and law professor Harlan Protass explains how the federal sentencing guidelines often punish white-collar criminals disproportionately:

Most big-time frauds are prosecuted in federal court, where the federal guidelines largely control sentencing. Using a complex set of calculations, those guidelines mechanically sort criminals into one of 43 "offense levels" based on different aspects of their crimes. Higher offense levels reflect more harmful conduct. They also give rise to longer prison terms. Offense-level assignment, in turn, is fixed largely by measuring ostensibly discernible quantities, such as the amount of drugs in a narcotics case or, in cases involving fraud, the amount of money lost. . . .

[W]hen it comes to large-scale frauds involving public companies and their millions of shares, the guidelines' grounding in mathematics sometimes results in sentences that are, quite literally, off the charts. They fall within the realm of prison terms usually reserved for Mafia bosses, major international drug lords, cop killers, child molesters, and terrorists.

Remember Jeffrey Skilling? Losses to Enron shareholders of more than $1 billion largely determined his 24-year-plus sentence. Or consider World-Com's former chief, Bernard J. Ebbers. He got 25 years based principally on the $2.2 billion loss suffered by his company's shareholders. Sure, these men destroyed enormous shareholder value, just as the targets of today's criminal cases allegedly did. But it's hard to contend that they deserved prison terms longer than the average sentence for murder (22 years), kidnapping (14), and sexual abuse (eight).

Source: Harlan J. Protass, "Even Bernard Madoff Doesn't Deserve This," *Washington Post*, December 21, 2008. http://www.washingtonpost.com/wp-dyn/content/article/2008/12/19/AR2008121903121.html.

wrote, "There is no real help, no real program to rehabilitate, no programs to educate, no way to be prepared for life 'out there' where each person will ultimately find herself, many with no skills and no preparation for living."[16]

Unfortunately, all of this seems to miss the point by focusing only on the criminals and their actions; the victims are not taken into account. In no other area is the benefit of keeping the offenders in society as great as in white-collar crimes. Instead of locking away these criminals, the system should allow them to use their professional expertise to make money so they can repay the people they cheated or stole from. A better approach would be to keep white-collar criminals responsible to make things right, rather than just shutting them out of society.[17]

Summary

Criminals should receive punishment, but what the appropriate punishment should be is often a harder question than first appears. White-collar crimes are nonviolent crimes that usually only cause financial harm. In an effort to remain fair, society must look at the real cost that white-collar criminals experience during their time in the penal system and realize that it is often unnecessarily harsh. Also, because these punishments already meet the goals of the criminal justice system, they should not be enhanced to meet the emotional needs of angry mobs. Finally, focusing on providing restoration to the victims is more helpful to society than locking away nonviolent, white-collar criminals.

Government Must Protect Citizens from White-Collar Crime

"There's got to be another explanation. I don't care how it looks. No one could do this."[1]

On July 27, 2001, a group of agents from the FBI and the Food and Drug Administration (FDA) sat around a conference table looking at stacks of papers from an evidence report. Despite being a hardened group of law enforcement professionals who had been trained to deal with all types of human deviance, they refused to believe what was before their eyes. Even as FBI agent Judy Lewis exclaimed her disbelief, the agents began to create an action plan to verify what was really happening.[2]

What caused such disbelief? It was a collection of evidence that Dr. Verda Hunter, an oncologist, had gathered on pharmacist Robert Courtney. She had used Courtney's pharmacy to fill chemotherapy prescriptions for some years. But after an offhand comment from a drug representative about the limited amount of drugs Courtney was purchasing, Hunter became suspicious. She tested one of the prescriptions Courtney had filled for a chemotherapy drug and discovered that the medication had been diluted. Courtney had been diluting chemotherapy medication to increase his profits. Such craven actions seemed beyond the capabilities of any regular person, and the reality of the situation made Hunter angry and sick.[3]

After receiving this evidence from Hunter, the FBI planned a sting operation to catch Courtney in the act. Over the next few days, Hunter ordered nine prescriptions from Courtney. When tested, most of the drugs contained only 17 to 39 percent of the medication they were supposed to include. One dose had only trace amounts of the prescription ordered. The trusted pharmacist was taken in handcuffs from the pharmacy as agents swarmed in to search for further evidence. Asked then if he could explain why the dosages were diluted, Courtney's only comment was: "No sir, I can't. I don't understand it."[4]

After his arrest, he admitted that he had begun to buy drugs off the gray market (distribution channels that, although legal, are unauthorized by the original manufacturer) in an effort to make enough money to pay his first wife the nearly $200,000 he agreed to in their divorce. After that, Courtney began to engage in ever more criminal acts, from substituting generic drugs for name brands to his most heinous crime, diluting medications. Over the course of a decade, he is believed to have diluted 98,000 prescriptions, affecting approximately 4,200 patients. Chemotherapy drugs were the most profitable, but he did not discriminate. He diluted 72 different drugs ranging from fertility drugs to antibiotics to clotting medications—anything that could be "compounded" or mixed in solution, he could find a way to cut and dilute. By the time he was caught, Courtney had amassed a personal fortune of almost $20 million. But no amount of money diminished his desire to accumulate more by stealing from those who trusted him with their most precious possession—their health.[5]

During his sentencing, victims came forward to give statements about the impact Courtney's crimes had on their lives. Mary Ann Rhoads, a cancer survivor who had received her chemotherapy drugs from Courtney, summed up the feeling in the room when she said she felt violated. In the end, Courtney received a 35-year sentence. For his victims, however, his actions amounted to a veritable death sentence. As part of his sentence, Courtney also lost his pharmacist's license and had to sell both of his pharmacies. Following the criminal trial, Courtney faced more than 300 civil lawsuits from his victims. The most troubling part of the ordeal, however, remains the questions left about who else may be tampering with the life-preserving drugs people take every day.[6]

Clearly it is the responsibility of the government to be involved in stopping such criminal behavior. One of the best ways to stop such wrongdoing is to provide oversight and regulation of industries and activities that are susceptible to white-collar criminal conduct. Providing such proactive oversight is part of the government's duty in protecting citizens. Such approaches are more ethical and more efficient at stopping abuses to those least able to protect themselves than allowing markets alone to regulate such conduct. Ultimately, strict regulation provides the greatest protection and the greatest benefits, especially when responding to the often-dispersed effects of white-collar crime.

The government has a duty to protect its citizens from white-collar criminals.

What role does the government play in keeping citizens safe, and how extensive should that role be? Every society must wrestle with this question of how to balance freedom and order. In the United States, freedom has historically been touted as of paramount interest. But this does not mean that citizens are willing to give up an ordered society to attain the greatest possible degree of freedom. Instead, the U.S. approach tends to be rather hands-off on most matters, but that changes when one person's actions affect another person.[7] As Justice Oliver Wendell Holmes Jr. once said, "The right to swing my fist ends where the other man's nose begins."[8] White-collar crime is particularly insidious because of how it is often perpetrated. Using their advanced expertise, superior power, or unique positions in the economic world, white-collar criminals are able to defraud and/or harm people in ways that the average person can hardly be expected to defend against.[9] When a pharmacist dilutes a patient's drug, there is no practical way for the patient to get the drugs checked or verified. When a company fails to provide necessary safety equipment, it is not likely to warn its workers that they are at an elevated risk for injury. And when a financier assures a trusting couple that their retirement money is being carefully invested,

QUOTABLE

Dean Baker, Co-Director of the Center for Economic and Policy Research

To be fair, rarely does either side argue against regulation as such. The real issue is the structure of regulation and its impact on economic outcomes, especially income distribution. . . .

In the decades preceding the financial collapse, regulations designed to protect the public and to ensure the stability of the financial system were considerably weakened, but the system was (and is) quite far from being deregulated.

The key regulation that remained in place was the "too-big-to-fail" doctrine. Essentially, the banks and other financial institutions took enormous risks with an implicit guarantee that their creditors could count on the protection of the U.S. government if things went badly. For everyone except the creditors of Lehman Brothers and the preferred shareholders of Fannie Mae and Freddie Mac, this gamble proved correct.

This one-sided giveaway was not deregulation. Had those setting financial policy over the last three decades been committed to deregulation, they would have assured financial markets that financial institutions making bad investments would go out of business and that their creditors would be out of luck. The Federal Reserve Board and the Treasury would have warned that investors were acting at their own risk when they put money in Bear Stearns, AIG, and the rest.

they have few resources to check on how their savings are actually being managed. In the case of Madoff, his company was the recipient of contracts with other companies that invested retirement accounts. Many people who lost money in the Madoff scam did not even know they were invested in his funds until after the Ponzi scheme was revealed and their accounts were decimated.[10]

Because of the specialized expertise involved in most white-collar crimes, it is all the more important that government agencies monitor and regulate businesses that are susceptible to white-collar crime. The government has the resources and enforcement power to look into possibly criminal situations and protect those who cannot protect themselves. As opposed to

In the context of a too-big-to-fail principle, the removal of [certain] restrictions and the relaxation of other prudential regulation essentially gave the banks a license to wager with taxpayers' money.

Banks did exactly what economic theory predicts. They took huge risks, leveraging themselves to the hilt with questionable assets, knowing that they would gain as long as the housing bubble held up. And the banks did so with willing accomplices among pension funds, hedge funds, and other investors because these investors knew that the government would rescue them if things went badly.

Deregulation can be a principled position held by true believers in a free market. But Wall Streeters all wanted one-sided regulation that provided them with an enormous government security blanket without any costs or conditions. None of the Citigroup, Goldman Sachs, J.P. Morgan crew ever went to lobby Congress for an explicit repeal of the too-big-to-fail doctrine. And while many on Wall Street lost their jobs when the bubble burst, the tens or hundreds of millions of dollars that banking executives earned during the good times are theirs to keep. Even with the market collapse, the vast majority of them are almost certainly better off than they would have been had they done honest work over the last decade.

Source: Dean Baker, "Free Market Myth," *Boston Review*, January/February 2009, http://bostonreview.net/BR34.1/baker.php.

street crime, where neighbors can look out for each other and neighborhood watches can decrease street-crime levels, white-collar crimes are not amenable to private and volunteer crime control.

Dangerous and harmful situations need proactive management.

Those who dislike government regulation often claim that laws and rules meant to stop white-collar and other crimes

THE LETTER OF THE LAW

Sarbanes-Oxley Act of 2002

In the wake of the Enron scandal of 2001–2002, Congress passed legislation to provide greater oversight and stiffer penalties for corporations and the professional firms that service them. Following is a short summary by the American Institute of Certified Public Accountants of some key provisions of the Sarbanes-Oxley Act:

Title VIII: Corporate and Criminal Fraud Accountability.

It is a felony to "knowingly" destroy or create documents to "impede, obstruct or influence" any existing or contemplated federal investigation.

Auditors are required to maintain "all audit or review work papers" for five years.

The statute of limitations on securities fraud claims is extended to the earlier of five years from the fraud, or two years after the fraud was discovered, from three years and one year, respectively.

Employees of issuers and accounting firms are extended "whistleblower protection" that would prohibit the employer from taking certain actions against employees who lawfully disclose private employer information to, among others, parties in a judicial proceeding involving a fraud claim. Whistleblowers are also granted a remedy of special damages and attorney's fees.

A new crime for securities fraud that has penalties of fines and up to 10 years imprisonment.

are intrusive and unnecessary. These "free-market" enthusi-asts attempt to portray government oversight of industry as a violation of the basic principles of capitalism and even basic freedoms. Instead of regulation, it is argued that the market will take care of problems such as those who abuse the system or otherwise commit criminal acts.[11]

But this is not the way the system works, nor is it ethical. While it is true that eventually people will find out about busi-nesses and people who harm others and avoid dealing with

Title IX: White-Collar Crime Penalty Enhancements.

Maximum penalty for mail and wire fraud increased from 5 to 10 years.

Creates a crime for tampering with a record or otherwise impeding any official proceeding.

SEC [is] given authority to seek court freeze of extraordinary payments to directors, offices, partners, controlling persons, agents of employees.

U.S. Sentencing Commission to review sentencing guidelines for securities and accounting fraud.

SEC may prohibit anyone convicted of securities fraud from being an officer or director of any publicly traded company.

Financial statements filed with the SEC must be certified by the CEO and CFO [chief financial officer]. The certification must state that the financial statements and disclosures fully comply with provisions of the Securities Exchange Act and that they fairly present, in all material respects, the oper-ations and financial condition of the issuer. Maximum penalties for willful and knowing violations of this section are a fine of not more than $500,000 and/or imprisonment of up to 5 years.

Source: "Summary of the Provisions of the Sarbanes-Oxley Act of 2002." AICPA. http://thecaq.aicpa.org/Resources/Sarbanes+Oxley/Summary+of+the+Provisions+of+the+Sarbanes-Oxley+Act+of+2002.htm#top.

them, those who are harmed in the meantime will find little solace or help. The reality is that society takes preventive measures to stop abuses all the time. Society does not allow "the market" to take care of street crimes. No one would agree to allow people to build methamphetamine labs in their homes, expecting the neighbors to move away from the danger so as not to interfere with the drug producers' freedom. Instead, citizens expect the government to proactively stop dangerous situations, like methamphetamine labs, from hurting unsuspecting neighbors.

Similarly, society should not expect people who are trying to invest their retirement money, work safely, or drink clean water to have to take care of these problems themselves. The government has an obligation to keep its citizens safe. When it comes to professional services, the government must take proactive measures that limit the possibility of loss from the acts of white-collar criminals. The problem with allowing "the market" to handle harmful situations is that it relies on solutions after the fact. Once a crime has been committed, it is often too late for those who were affected. An elderly couple finds little solace in being able to sue after all of their retirement money has been embezzled. The years it takes a civil suit to work its way through the court system could mean too little, too late for many. In instances such as a pharmacist diluting drugs, the victims could die before they are able to get any relief. This is a hefty societal cost to pay just so individuals and companies can make as much money as possible with the least amount of regulation or interference.

Regulation can prevent harms to the greatest numbers.

One of the greatest problems with white-collar crime is that the damaging effects are often spread over a large number of people. Because the losses are rather small to each individual, they often go unnoticed. Even when people do notice abnormalities or problems, they are usually so tiny that they are not worth reporting to the police. As such, great harms may be perpetrated on society, but they are never set right because no one person has been hurt enough to take action.[12]

That is one of the reasons that government regulation is so much better at dealing with white-collar crimes than individual self-help. In 2003, the White House Office of Management and Budget created the first-ever report on the costs and benefits of federal regulation. The main finding was clear and unequivocal—regulation is well worth the cost to taxpayers. The report found that while regulation costs taxpayers $38 billion to $44 billion a year, the benefits amount to $135 billion to $218 billion.[13] These benefits include keeping companies liable for pollution they may create and ensuring that it does not end up in drinking water or the air. In other industries, the benefits include requiring employers to provide safety equipment and training for employees so they are not hurt at work. In other instances, it can include oversight of the finance industry, making sure that investments are appropriately handled, and that investors have more protections from those who try to steal. Given the numbers, regulation seems to be a good return on investment for society.[14]

Summary

White-collar crime is a problem that requires a concerted response by government. Part of the government's job is to make sure that citizens are protected from criminals. One of the most effective ways that government can do that in the context of white-collar crime is to make sure that businesses and individuals susceptible to white-collar crime are regulated and given the oversight needed to protect society. While this may not provide the market solutions that some prefer, it does provide the greatest benefit to the largest number of people in society. These benefits are also provided at relatively little cost, especially when compared with the benefits received.

Government Regulation of White-Collar Crime Is Ineffective

With $20.6 billion in net sales in 2008 and with facilities in 13 countries, Bristol-Myers Squibb (BMS) is one of the largest pharmaceutical companies in the world. Its work affects hundreds of thousands of lives each year and their products help many people. Plavix, a blood-thinning medicine that helps prevent heart attacks and strokes, and Abilify, an antipsychotic medication with numerous uses, are just two of the company's popular medications.[1] Such a company is not used to being told what to do or how to do it, but on June 15, 2005, BMS entered into a bizarre agreement, giving complete oversight of the company to one man, U.S. Attorney Christopher Christie, who would be elected governor of New Jersey in November 2009.[2]

The problems had begun months and even years earlier. BMS had engaged in possible criminal activities involving incentives for distributors to buy more product than they needed in

prosecution agreements to go beyond what is reasonable or just in a given situation and push for more.[10]

Criminal prosecution, however, is not always the best solution to many of these problems. Often, the criminal justice system is poorly equipped to deal with white-collar activities. Market forces often work better at generating solutions. By allowing people to work within the markets, with private individuals or government agencies suing when companies cause harm, the greatest amount of freedom and benefits accrue to both companies and consumers. Especially in modern environments, where information is omnipresent, markets have never had a better opportunity to self-regulate against abuses and crimes than ever before.[11]

Increased criminalization of white-collar acts creates more harm than good for the public.

One of the greatest problems with the current system of policing white-collar crime is the collateral damage these policies cause. This is primarily seen in the methods of enforcement and in the misallocation of limited resources. Both result in innocent citizens being harmed, economically and possibly physically.

Enforcement schemes cause wide collateral damage. As was seen in the Arthur Andersen situation, criminal charges and prosecutions caused irrevocable damages. Damages were not limited to the CEO or even a few rogue employees. The entire firm, which had revenues of $9.3 billion before the collapse of Enron in 2001, was shut down.[12] Thirty-thousand employees lost their jobs. Clients from around the world were thrown into chaos as they had to switch to new accounting firms. What was Arthur Andersen's crime? According to the Supreme Court—nothing.[13]

Even the act of prosecuting crimes is often far more expensive than the criminal harm itself. In the case of Martha Stewart, the questionable stock deal she was supposed to have been involved in was worth about $51,000. Before it was over, Stewart's legal expenses alone exceeded $3.7 million.[14] This is to say nothing of the cost to the government for staff time, expert witnesses, and other requirements of prosecution.

Some may argue that these expenses are reasonable, especially if it stops crime. But is it really? Millions of dollars spent on prosecuting people for rather minor activities seems disproportionate. And for people who find it hard to find much sympathy for millionaires, it is important to remember that ultimately the cost of prosecuting these kinds of activities falls back on taxpayers and consumers. With the police in dangerous neighborhoods often understaffed and underequipped, money

QUOTABLE

Ellen S. Podgor

Ellen S. Podgor of Stetson University College of Law wrote a letter to future politicians describing how the government used the Arthur Andersen/Enron situation to create a system that seems less than fair:

Enron was never indicted although individuals within the company were indicted. But the government then decided to indict the accounting firm associated with Enron. The company was shredding documents right and left, so the government decided to hit them with charges of obstruction of justice. Well the company decided to go to trial. After all, the sentence was a maximum fine of $500,000. What did they have to lose? The funny, but not so funny thing, is that they lost the initial trial, the company went under, people in offices throughout the world lost their jobs because of the indictment, and then they won in the United States Supreme Court. The problem was that the company was already dead. Once executed, there was not much that could be done. The number of major accounting firms in the U.S. was decreased by one, all because they failed to plead guilty or cooperate with the government. . . .

The result of all this was that anytime the government even raised a finger that they might be considering indicting a company, the company was on the doorstep of the government, offering them everything. Companies became mini-prosecutors for the government, giving tabbed notebooks

should clearly be spent on physical safety before prosecutors go after what often turn out to be victimless crimes.[15]

Attempts at stopping all white-collar crime limits freedom for all.

Cost of enforcement, especially when compared with the actual harms done, is clearly a point of concern. But for many people, the greater concern has to do with the erosion of freedom for all people implicit in criminalizing corporate and business activities. In some cases, people are limited in the kinds of

of information to the government about employees in order to get them to stop indicting their company. More companies entered into deferred prosecution agreements during these times than had ever done so before. Companies were dropping millions of dollars and saying they would give the government everything they needed to prosecute individuals in their office, as long as the government assured them that they would not be indicted like Arthur Andersen.

You can't blame the companies for being nervous, as Arthur Andersen— a losing case—became the biggest deterrent the government could ever have. "Cooperate or we execute" was the government's mantra. In these deferred prosecution agreements they even made the corporation agree that they would not pay the attorney fees of individuals in the company, even if the corporate employee and the corporation had a contract for the payment of these fees.

Some of these agreements were beyond belief. For example, in one agreement with Bristol-Myers Squibb Company, the government and the company agreed to put an ethics chair at Seton Hall Law School. Yes, this was right in the agreement. And lo and behold, the United States attorney that entered into the agreement with the company graduated from Seton Hall Law School.

Source: Ellen S. Podgor, "White-Collar Crime: A Letter from the Future," *Ohio State Journal of Criminal Law.* 97:731 (2007): p. 247.

activities and economic relationships they may engage in, even if no one else is hurt or involved. In more nefarious situations, even fundamental rights are put in jeopardy.

One example of how attempts at detecting and limiting white-collar crime can restrict a person's freedom has to do with

FROM THE BENCH

Arthur Anderson v. the United States, 544 U.S. 696 (2005)

As Enron Corporation's financial difficulties became public in 2001, petitioner Arthur Andersen LLP, Enron's auditor, instructed its employees to destroy documents pursuant to its document retention policy. A jury found that this action made petitioner guilty of violating 18 U.S.C. §§ 1512(b)(2)(A) and (B). These sections make it a crime to "knowingly use intimidation or physical force, threaten, or corruptly persuade another person . . . with intent to . . . cause" that person to "withhold" documents from, or "alter" documents for use in, an "official proceeding." . . . We hold that the jury instructions failed to convey properly the elements of a "corrup[t] persua[sion]" conviction under § 1512(b), and therefore reverse. . . .

[T]he witness tampering provisions, provide in relevant part:

"Whoever knowingly uses intimidation or physical force, threatens, or corruptly persuades another person, or attempts to do so, or engages in misleading conduct toward another person, with intent to . . . cause or induce any person to . . . withhold testimony, or withhold a record, document, or other object, from an official proceeding [or] alter, destroy, mutilate, or conceal an object with intent to impair the object's integrity or availability for use in an official proceeding . . . shall be fined under this title or imprisoned not more than ten years, or both."

In this case, our attention is focused on what it means to "knowingly . . . corruptly persuade" another person "with intent to . . . cause" that person to "withhold" documents from, or "alter" documents for use in, an "official proceeding."

We have traditionally exercised restraint in assessing the reach of a federal criminal statute. . . . Such restraint is particularly appropriate here, where the act underlying the conviction—"persuasion"—is by itself innocuous. Indeed, "persuading" a person "with intent to . . . cause" that person to "withhold" testimony

pharmaceutical testing. The Food and Drug Administration (FDA) requires years of testing and review before a drug is allowed on the market. These rules prohibit any human use until the trials are completed. Intending to keep citizens safe, the FDA limits the ability of those who are grievously ill or

or documents from a Government proceeding or Government official is not inherently malign. Consider, for instance, a mother who suggests to her son that he invoke his right against compelled self-incrimination, or a wife who persuades her husband not to disclose marital confidences. Nor is it necessarily corrupt for an attorney to "persuade" a client "with intent to . . . cause" that client to "withhold" documents from the Government. . . .

"Document retention policies," which are created in part to keep certain information from getting into the hands of others, including the Government, are common in business. It is, of course, not wrongful for a manager to instruct his employees to comply with a valid document retention policy under ordinary circumstances. . . .

[T]he jury instructions at issue simply failed to convey the requisite consciousness of wrongdoing. Indeed, it is striking how little culpability the instructions required. For example, the jury was told that, "even if [petitioner] honestly and sincerely believed that its conduct was lawful, you may find [petitioner] guilty." The instructions also diluted the meaning of "corruptly" so that it covered innocent conduct. . . .

The instructions also were infirm for another reason. They led the jury to believe that it did not have to find any nexus between the "persuasion" to destroy documents and any particular proceeding. . . . It is, however, one thing to say that a proceeding "need not be pending or about to be instituted at the time of the offense," and quite another to say a proceeding need not even be foreseen. A "knowingly . . . corrupt persuader" cannot be someone who persuades others to shred documents under a document retention policy when he does not have in contemplation any particular official proceeding in which those documents might be material. . . .

For these reasons, the jury instructions here were flawed in important respects. The judgment of the Court of Appeals is reversed, and the case is remanded for further proceedings consistent with this opinion.

dying to try new medications before it is too late. If a patient is willing to take the risks, why should the government be allowed to stop them?[16]

The other problem arises from the fact that white-collar crime is notoriously hard to detect and prosecute. Because of these barriers to enforcing the law, prosecutors are tempted to use ever more stringent measures to achieve prosecutions and compliance. In some instances, this leads to overreaching, as seen with BMS and the deferred prosecution agreement it was forced into.[17]

Another incident that appalled many in the legal system involved the accounting firm KPMG. Prosecutors were trying to build a case against accountants at the firm for creating tax shelters that allowed clients to avoid paying billions of dollars in taxes. Part of their strategy was to intimidate KPMG into not paying the legal fees for these accountants, even though KPMG was contractually obligated to do so. These tactics so outraged Judge Lewis Kaplan that he dismissed the case against 13 of the accountants.[18] In his written opinion, he explained that "[t]hose who commit crimes—regardless of whether they wear white or blue collars—must be brought to justice. The government, however, has let its zeal get in the way of its judgment. It has violated the Constitution it is sworn to defend."[19]

Summary
White-collar crimes can be harmful and should be taken seriously. But current methods of dealing with white-collar crime are neither ethical nor effective in many ways. The current system, and the desire by some to expand it, leads to excessive costs to companies and individuals alike. It violates the freedom of individuals to engage in desired activities, even when such activities harm no one else. Worst of all, the current system tempts prosecutors to take liberties with fundamental rights and basic ideas of fairness and justice.

The Future of White-Collar Crime

In the wake of the 2008–2009 financial distress in the United States and across the globe, many people clamored for tighter regulation, harsher penalties for fraud, and better supervision of the markets. It is easy to understand the sense of outrage, particularly when one looks at the shady practices that led to the economic recession: Bernard Madoff's scheme that caused many to question how safe retirement accounts really were.[1] The housing bubble bursting because of lax requirements on home loans.[2] Major U.S. industries nearly collapsed because of poor business decisions.[3] The question remains, are these really white-collar crimes?

This question has been asked since Edwin Sutherland first brought up the concept of white-collar crime back in the 1930s. It is a question that will vex scholars and law enforcement officials alike for years to come. In the previous examples, Madoff's fraud was clearly a white-collar crime that virtually everyone agrees deserved criminal sanctions. But what about the financial industry and industrial production companies? Did their actions rise to the level of a crime? Their actions harmed far more people than Madoff's crimes did, resulting in global economic shock waves and a vast economic recession.

The standard for what is and is not a white-collar crime is not likely to get any easier. With improvements in technology, the crimes of today may look nothing like the crimes of tomorrow. Technology will affect not only how the crimes are

---

QUOTABLE

A Former Fraudster Speaks Out: Sam E. Antar, former CPA and CFO of Crazy Eddie Inc.

Sam E. Antar perpetrated a fraud on investors that ultimately cost hundreds of millions of dollars. Antar was instrumental, along with his cousin, Eddie, and his uncle, Sam M. Antar, in creating the scheme. Here, he speaks about white-collar crime:

A white-collar criminal carries a lethal weapon that . . . can be in many ways more lethal than a gun. The white-collar criminal's weapon is the intellect within his mind.

White-collar criminals cannot be profiled, since according to most studies over 90 percent of them have no previous criminal records. Worst yet, the criminals who commit securities fraud and financial statement fraud almost never have previous criminal records.

White-collar crime is a crime of persuasion. It is a crime committed with a smile rather than a gun. Many white-collar criminals are likable people. They use their personality as a tool. They use your humanity, personality, and good intentions against you. White-collar criminals consider your good traits such as goodwill and trust as "weaknesses to be exploited" in the execution of their crimes.

Criminals are capable of doing good deeds while they are involved in their criminal acts. For example, many convicted felons were involved

committed but also how they are investigated. Policy makers will continue to struggle with appropriately defining criminal responsibility, especially as companies are increasingly left to struggle between doing what is legal and doing what is ethical. Finally, the underrepresented element of white-collar crimes will need to be addressed in the future—the victims. New ways will have to be devised to take victims into account. Prosecution of criminals is not enough. Making sure the victims receive restitution and restoration will become the greatest of future struggles.

in charity work during the same period of time that they were committing their crimes. Good deeds in one area of their lives do not prevent a person from being a criminal in another area of their lives.

Criminals try to avoid accountability by showcasing their good deeds. Crimes cannot be excused and scrutiny stopped because of the good deeds people have done in other areas of their lives.

In fact, an important tool of a white-collar criminal is your gratitude. White-collar criminals hope that their "good deeds" will weaken your defenses, professional skepticism, objectivity, and inquiry into their actions. They hope that one day you may come to their aid and publicly defend them. White-collar criminals build a wall of false integrity around them by showcasing their good deeds, while living a parallel life of crime.

White-collar criminals commit crimes simply because "they can." They commit their crimes simply because the incentive and opportunity is available to them.

The most effective way to reduce white-collar crime is by prevention. We must create barriers such as strong internal controls. Such internal controls must be reviewed by competent, educated, skilled, experienced, and truly independent external auditors.

We need to move toward a more pre-emptive approach to white-collar crime. We cannot hope to significantly prevent or reduce white-collar crime by relying on the threat of long prison terms for convicted felons.

Source: http://www.whitecollarfraud.com/index.html.

Technology will continue to change the face of white-collar crime.

Author Terry Leap writes in his book *Dishonest Dollars*:

> In the future, the mix of white-collar crime is likely to change. There are two major crimes that may increase: health-care fraud and crimes that use computer technology. . . . Computer technology and the Internet will continue to provide a springboard for white-collar crime. . . . Telemarketing fraud may decrease as consumers become increasingly wary of cold calls from strangers, but Internet-based consumer fraud may increase.[4]

While technology-related crimes are likely to increase, the good news is that other white-collar crimes will likely decrease. Due to the increased number of laws overseeing financial markets, especially Sarbanes-Oxley, insider trading and other financial frauds are likely to decrease. These new laws and more stringent accounting standards will make it increasingly harder to hide money or engage in fraudulent practices. Also, copyright and trademark infringements, as well as counterfeit goods, are likely to decrease due to increased cooperation between the U.S. and other governments, especially China.[5]

Investigation of white-collar crime will change.

As newspapers close across the country, one of the crucial watchdogs of white-collar crime may be lost with them. The dispersed effect of many white-collar crimes often leads individuals to write them off. If victims lose only a few dollars, or even a few hundred, they may not feel that the crime is worth reporting to authorities. While the individual may only be harmed a little, the number of victims may result in a rather large loss to society as a whole. This is where community watchdogs, such as local newspapers, can serve such an important function. Without someone watching, no one individual will have enough vested interest to bring these situations to light.[6]

FBI caseload

The FBI has sent fewer cases to federal prosecutors since the Sept. 11 terror attacks. How the caseloads have changed:

		Cases sent to		New investigation	
Overall	2000	11,029		N/	
	2003	9,351 ▼	-15%	N/	
Drugs	2001	2,994		1,447	
	2003	1,840 ▼	-40%	58 ▼	-60%
White collar crime	2001	6,941		20,036	
	2003	5,331 ▼	-23%	13,531 ▼	-32%
Violent crime	2001	5,003		30,601	
	2003	4,491 ▼	-10%	18,455 ▼	-40%
Terrorism	2001	23		1,006	
	2003	1,821 ▲	+671%	2,850 ▲	+183%

Note: All data is for fiscal years

Source: U.S. Attorney's Annual Statistical reports, U.S. Government Accountability Office
Graphic: Judy Treible, Tim Goheen   © 2004 KRT

The FBI sent fewer criminal cases to U.S. attorneys for prosecution, including cases related to white-collar crimes, between 2000 and 2003, with the exception of terrorism cases.

Newspapers and investigative reports have historically served in this function. Although print journalism is suffering economic losses, the journalistic spirit does not seem to be diminishing. Without the startup costs and overhead of a print newspaper, many amateurs, and even some professionals, have turned their talents to the Web. Through blogs and personal Web pages, individual citizens can now take on the role of watchdogs in their communities. The future of white-collar crime will likely be intricately tied to the Internet and social networking, with the vast communication and information-sharing abilities they provide. The shared information allows those who are affected by white-collar criminals to compare stories, warn one another of threats, and collect victim's information for law enforcement.

An Excerpt from the FBI's White-Collar Crime Strategic Plan

Since the 1990s, tremendous growth of and involvement in the securities and commodities markets at the institutional, corporate, and private investor levels have led to great numbers of individuals involved in intentional corporate fraud and misconduct, particularly senior corporate executives. For example, the FBI is currently investigating over 189 major corporate frauds, 18 of which have losses over $1 billion. The erosion of public confidence in the management of public companies will, if left unchecked, have a negative impact on the stock markets and capital raising, which will in turn have a negative impact throughout the U.S. economy.

Health-care fraud continues to plague the United States, with losses exceeding $50 billion annually. Frauds involving durable medical equipment, staged auto accidents, and medical transportation services are examples of this pervasive crime problem. In addition to Medicare/Medicaid and private insurers, state providers lose billions of dollars per year to blatant fraud schemes in every sector of the health-care industry. As health-care spending increases over the coming years with the aging of the "baby boom" generation and Medicare prescription drug coverage, health-care fraud is expected to have a corresponding increase.

Financial institution fraud (FIF) continues to be a significant white-collar crime problem throughout the country. Since 9/11, the FBI has refocused its FIF program and is now investigating higher-priority cases to a much greater degree. Large-scale mortgage fraud and identity theft operations, many perpetrated by organized criminal enterprises, also continue to plague the United States.

Aggressive use of anti-money laundering statutes and forfeiture of ill-gotten assets are integral parts of nearly every financial crime prosecution. Many top

Future policy makers will have to balance legality and ethics.

While new technologies will always provide new means of criminality along with new means of detection, one of the most contentious areas of future discussions on white-collar crime is

executives involved in corporate scandals have been charged with money laundering in addition to other criminal violations. Additionally, corrupt money launderers introduce illegal proceeds into the financial community, and this asset flow must be reduced through aggressive prosecution, seizure, and forfeiture.

The ability of the U.S. Government and industry to function effectively is likewise threatened by complex frauds. The amount of taxpayer funds involved in the government procurement process is staggering, as billions of dollars are spent each year on everything from highways to rockets. The GAO [Government Accountability Office] estimates that as much as 10 percent of appropriated funds for domestic programs may be lost to fraud in the government procurement and contracting process, and this type of crime is critically linked to public corruption imperatives.

Insurance, telemarketing, and investment frauds often operate across jurisdictional and international boundaries. When losses to individual victims are aggregated, the economic impact can be dramatic. Additionally, anti-trust offenses and bankruptcy fraud have a significant negative effect on the U.S. economy, and environmental crimes represent a serious threat to the public health and natural resources of our nation.

The FBI will continue its successful efforts in the white-collar crime arena by using its expertise, broad criminal investigative resources, and strong relationships with regulatory agencies to maintain public confidence in the country's financial institutions and markets, ensure the integrity of government expenditures of taxpayer funds, and protect individuals and businesses from catastrophic economic loss.

Source: "Federal Bureau of Investigation Strategic Plan 2004–2009: White-Collar Crime." http://www.fbi.gov/publications/strategicplan/stategicplantext.htm#whitecollar.

the same as it has always been. Future generations will have to engage in and struggle with the unintended consequences that result from legislation designed to frustrate white-collar crime. Balancing efficiency, effectiveness, morality, ethics, and capability will continue to be the struggle for decades to come.

One problem in particular is the balance between ethics and legality. While counterintuitive, many scholars point out that one of the greatest problems with the ever-growing web of activities that are now considered criminal is that they lead to less compliance. In some cases, managers are put in the unenviable position of choosing between the most ethical course of action and the most legal. In some cases, companies know that an employee is innocent, yet legal incentives have been created that reward the company with lower fines if they cooperate with the government in trying to prosecute an innocent employee. If they fail to provide evidence against an employee they know to be innocent, managers could expose their company to greater fines and punishments. Since they have a duty to protect the company, these managers are required to act unethically, to remain legal.[7]

More focus will have to be on victims' rights and restoration.

As has historically been the case, most criminal scholarship and policy decisions have focused on the criminal. The only real examination of the victim is found in how badly the victim is harmed by the criminal's activity, usually for the purposes of determining just punishment. But new avenues of research and legislation have provided for concepts like restorative justice to emerge as a way of addressing the victims of crimes. Often this requires the criminals to help right the wrongs they committed and be confronted by the people they hurt.[8]

Victims' rights groups have also been formed around the country to lobby for more attention to be paid to the needs of victims throughout the prosecutorial process and the sentencing that follows. The U.S. Department of Justice set up the Office for Victims of Crimes in 1984. This office is designed to connect victims with the resources they need to help them deal with the problems they face.[9] These types of initiatives are likely to increase in the future, and the questions and controversies over how they will affect law enforcement will continue for generations to come.

Summary

White-collar crime has been one of the most controversial areas of the criminal justice system for decades. From its inception, white-collar crime has been controversial in its definition and scope, as well as in determining the best ways to combat it. Whether Dr. Sutherland could have imagined the likes of Bernard Madoff, or the level of economic havoc he wreaked on families and institutions alike, no one may ever know. But now that the idea of white-collar crime is embedded in the national conscience, the controversies surrounding it are here to stay. The question now is which white-collar criminals next will gain the title of the "greatest scoundrels, thieves, liars, criminals," and what legal methods will be available to catch them.[10]

Beginning Legal Research

The goals of each book in the POINT/COUNTERPOINT series are not only to give the reader a basic introduction to a controversial issue affecting society, but also to encourage the reader to explore the issue more fully. This Appendix is meant to serve as a guide to the reader in researching the current state of the law as well as exploring some of the public policy arguments as to why existing laws should be changed or new laws are needed.

Although some sources of law can be found primarily in law libraries, legal research has become much faster and more accessible with the advent of the Internet. This Appendix discusses some of the best starting points for free access to laws and court decisions, but surfing the Web will uncover endless additional sources of information. Before you can research the law, however, you must have a basic understanding of the American legal system.

The most important source of law in the United States is the Constitution. Originally enacted in 1787, the Constitution outlines the structure of our federal government, as well as setting limits on the types of laws that the federal government and state governments can enact. Through the centuries, a number of amendments have added to or changed the Constitution, most notably the first 10 amendments, which collectively are known as the "Bill of Rights" and which guarantee important civil liberties.

Reading the plain text of the Constitution provides little information. For example, the Constitution prohibits "unreasonable searches and seizures" by the police. To understand concepts in the Constitution, it is necessary to look to the decisions of the U.S. Supreme Court, which has the ultimate authority in interpreting the meaning of the Constitution. For example, the U.S. Supreme Court's 2001 decision in *Kyllo v. United States* held that scanning the outside of a person's house using a heat sensor to determine whether the person is growing marijuana is an unreasonable search—if it is done without first getting a search warrant from a judge. Each state also has its own constitution and a supreme court that is the ultimate authority on its meaning.

Also important are the written laws, or "statutes," passed by the U.S. Congress and the individual state legislatures. As with constitutional provisions, the U.S. Supreme Court and the state supreme courts are the ultimate authorities in interpreting the meaning of federal and state laws, respectively. However, the U.S. Supreme Court might find that a state law violates the U.S. Constitution, and a state supreme court might find that a state law violates either the state or U.S. Constitution.

Not every controversy reaches either the U.S. Supreme Court or the state supreme courts, however. Therefore, the decisions of other courts are also important. Trial courts hear evidence from both sides and make a decision, while appeals courts review the decisions made by trial courts. Sometimes rulings from appeals courts are appealed further to the U.S. Supreme Court or the state supreme courts.

Lawyers and courts refer to statutes and court decisions through a formal system of citations. Use of these citations reveals which court made the decision or which legislature passed the statute, and allows one to quickly locate the statute or court case online or in a law library. For example, the Supreme Court case *Brown v. Board of Education* has the legal citation 347 U.S. 483 (1954). At a law library, this 1954 decision can be found on page 483 of volume 347 of the U.S. Reports, which are the official collection of the Supreme Court's decisions. On the following page, you will find samples of all the major kinds of legal citation.

Finding sources of legal information on the Internet is relatively simple thanks to "portal" sites such as findlaw.com and lexisone.com, which allow the user to access a variety of constitutions, statutes, court opinions, law review articles, news articles, and other useful sources of information. For example, findlaw.com offers access to all Supreme Court decisions since 1893. Other useful sources of information include gpo.gov, which contains a complete copy of the U.S. Code, and thomas.loc.gov, which offers access to bills pending before Congress, as well as recently passed laws. Of course, the Internet changes every second of every day, so it is best to do some independent searching.

Of course, many people still do their research at law libraries, some of which are open to the public. For example, some state governments and universities offer the public access to their law collections. Law librarians can be of great assistance, as even experienced attorneys need help with legal research from time to time.

Common Citation Forms

Source of Law	Sample Citation	Notes
U.S. Supreme Court	*Employment Division v. Smith*, 485 U.S. 660 (1988)	The U.S. Reports is the official record of Supreme Court decisions. There is also an unofficial Supreme Court ("S. Ct.") reporter.
U.S. Court of Appeals	*United States v. Lambert*, 695 F.2d 536 (11th Cir.1983)	Appellate cases appear in the Federal Reporter, designated by "F." The 11th Circuit has jurisdiction in Alabama, Florida, and Georgia.
U.S. District Court	*Carillon Importers, Ltd. v. Frank Pesce Group, Inc.*, 913 F.Supp. 1559 (S.D.Fla.1996)	Federal trial-level decisions are reported in the Federal Supplement ("F. Supp."). Some states have multiple federal districts; this case originated in the Southern District of Florida.
U.S. Code	Thomas Jefferson Commemoration Commission Act, 36 U.S.C., §149 (2002)	Sometimes the popular names of legislation—names with which the public may be familiar—are included with the U.S. Code citation.
State Supreme Court	*Sterling v. Cupp*, 290 Ore. 611, 614, 625 P.2d 123, 126 (1981)	The Oregon Supreme Court decision is reported in both the state's reporter and the Pacific regional reporter.
State Statute	Pennsylvania Abortion Control Act of 1982, 18 Pa. Cons. Stat. 3203-3220 (1990)	States use many different citation formats for their statutes.

Cases

Arthur Andersen v. United States, 544 U.S. 696 (May 31, 2005)

The Supreme Court overturned a lower court conviction that found the accounting firm Arthur Andersen guilty of obstructing justice by shredding documents related to the Enron Corporation. While this provided a symbolic victory for Andersen, it did nothing to revive the company that had nearly folded by the time the conviction was overturned.

United States v. Jeffrey Stein, et. al., S1 05 0888, Southern District of New York, (June 26, 2006)

This 88-page opinion by District Judge Lewis Kaplan threw out the charges against employees of the KPMG accounting firm. Judge Kaplan expressed concern that the deferred prosecution agreement that KPMG had entered into with the Justice Department violated the rights of the defendants because the agreement forbade KPMG to pay for legal counsel for the employees in question, despite contractual obligations requiring this support.

Statutes

Sarbanes-Oxley Act of 2002

In the wake of the Enron meltdown and other corporate collapses in 2000 and 2001, Congress passed the Sarbanes-Oxley Act in an effort to improve accountability and transparency in companies. The new rules required massive overhauls of accounting requirements and made certain members of management personally liable when they approved certain financial statements.

Terms and Concepts

Criminal intent

Criminologist

Deferred prosecution

Market forces

Ponzi scheme

Securities and Exchange Commission

Street crime

White-collar crime

NOTES

NOTES

Introduction: White-Collar Crime in the United States

1 "Elie Wiesel Says He Can't Forgive Bernie Madoff." CNN.com, February 27, 2009. Available online. URL: http://www.cnn.com/2009/CRIME/02/27/wiesel.madoff/.

2 Ibid.

3 Ibid.

4 "Madoff's Victims." *Wall Street Journal*, February 5, 2009. Available online. URL: http://s.wsj.net/public/resources/documents/st_madoff_victims_20081215.html.

5 Associated Press, "Ex-Financier Madoff Pleads Guilty to All Charges," MSNBC.com, March 12, 2009. Available online. URL: http://www.msnbc.msn.com/id/29651773/.

6 Gilbert Geis, *White-Collar and Corporate Crime.* Upper Saddle River, N.J.: Pearson Education, 2007, pp. 1–2.

7 Ibid., p. 2.

8 Gordon Marshall, "Crime," *A Dictionary of Sociology*, 1998, Encyclopedia.com, May 13, 2009. Available online. URL: http://www.encyclopedia.com.

9 Henry Campbell Black, "Crime," *Black's Law Dictionary*, 7th ed. St. Paul, Minn.: West Publishing, 1999.

10 Alfred H. Knight, *The Life of the Law.* New York: Crown Publishers, 1996, pp. 13–15.

11 Stuart Green, "The Concept of White Collar Crime in Law and Legal Theory," *Buffalo Criminal Law Review.* 8:1 (2005): pp. 2–3.

12 Edwin H. Sutherland, *White Collar Crime: The Uncut Version.* New Haven, Conn.: Yale University Press, 1983, p. 7.

13 Green, "The Concept of White Collar Crime in Law and Legal Theory," pp. 2–3.

14 "Facts and Figures 2003: White-Collar Crime," Federal Bureau of Investigation. Available online. URL: http://www.fbi.gov/libref/factsfigure/wcc.htm.

15 Ibid.

16 Exodus 20:15-16, *Holy Bible*, New Revised Standard Version. *Qu-ran*, 61.2-3.

17 Henry N. Pontell, "White Collar Crime and Major Financial Debacles in the United States," *Resource Materials Series*, no. 67, United Nations Asia and Far East Institute for the Prevention of Crime and Treatment of Offenders, December 2005. Available online. URL: http://www.unafei.or.jp/english/pdf/PDF_rms/no67/15_Pontell_p189-p201.pdf.

18 Antonello Biagioli, "Financial Crime as a Threat to the Wealth of Nations: A Cost-Effectiveness Approach," *Journal of Money Laundering Control.* 1:11 (2008): pp. 88–95.

19 David O. Friedrichs, *Trusted Criminals: White Collar Crime in Contemporary Society*, 3rd ed. Belmont, Calif.: Thomson/Wadsworth, 2007, pp. 1–30.

20 NPR Radio, "From Milken to Madoff: White-Collar Crime in Focus," NPR News and Notes, January 8, 2009. Available online. URL: http://www.npr.org/templates/story/story.php?storyId=99120924.

21 Jennifer S. Recine, "Examination of the White Collar Crime Penalty Enhancements in the Sarbanes-Oxley Act," *American Criminal Law Review.* 39:1535 (Fall 2002).

Point: Too Many Activities Are Considered White-Collar Crimes

1 18 United States Code 1512(c).

2 Christopher R. Chase, "To Shred or Not to Shred: Document Retention Policies and Federal Obstruction of Justice Statutes," *Fordham Journal of Corporate & Financial Law.* 8:721 (2003): pp. 740–743; Albert D. Spalding Jr. and Mary Ashbey Morrison,

"Criminal Liability for Document Shredding after Arthur Andersen, LLP," *American Business Law Journal*. 43:647 (2006): pp. 648–650.

3 Clyde Wayne Crews, "Ten Thousand Commandments 2009," Competitive Enterprise Institute, May 28, 2009. Available online. URL: http://cei.org/issue-analysis/2009/05/28/ten-thousand-commandments.

4 Fareed Zakaria, "A Capitalist Manifesto: Greed Is Good (to a Point)," *Newsweek*, June 13, 2009. Available online. URL: http://www.newsweek.com/id/201935.

5 Nance Lucas, "An Interview with United States Senator Paul S. Sarbanes," *Journal of Leadership & Organizational Studies*, Summer 2004. Available online. URL: http://findarticles.com/p/articles/mi_m0NXD/is_1_11/ai_n25101748/?tag=content;col1.

6 Joseph A. Grundfest and Steven E. Bochner, "Fixing 404," *Michigan Law Review*. 105:1643 (2007).

7 John Berlau, "Freedom and Its Digital Discontents," *The Economist*, March 17, 2008. Available online. URL: http://cei.org/articles/freedom-and-its-digital-discontents.

8 John S. Baker Jr., "The Sociological Origins of 'White Collar Crime'," *Legal Memorandum #14*, The Heritage Foundation, October 4, 2004. Available online. URL: http://www.heritage.org/research/legalissues/lm14.cfm.

9 Ibid.

10 Johnnie Roberts, "Do the Media Hate the Rich?" *Newsweek*, June 12, 2009. Available online. URL: http://www.newsweek.com/id/201864.

Counterpoint: More Activities Should Be Classified as White-Collar Crimes

1 Brigitte Yuille, "Child Identity Theft: A Victim's Story," Bankrate.com,

January 3, 2007. Available online. URL: http://www.bankrate.com/brm/news/debt/20070103_child_identity_theft_f1.asp.

2 "The Story of Bronti Kelly," MyIDfix.com. Available online. URL: http://www.myidfix.com/identity-theft-stories.php.

3 "Madoff Investor Found Dead in Apparent Suicide," CNN.com, December 24, 2008. Available online. URL: http://www.cnn.com/2008/CRIME/12/23/madoff.investor.suicide/index.html; Rachel Williams, "Madoff Fraud Victim Killed Himself to Avoid Bankruptcy," *Guardian*, June 11, 2009. Available online. URL: http://www.guardian.co.uk/uk/2009/jun/11/madoff-victim-suicide.

4 Andrea Schoepfer and Nicole Leeper Piquero, "Studying the Correlates of Fraud Victimization and Reporting," *Journal of Criminal Justice*. 37 (2009): p. 209.

5 Friedrichs, *Trusted Criminals*, pp. 52–53.

6 Ibid.

7 Schoepfer, "Studying the Correlates of Fraud Victimization and Reporting."

8 Yuille, "Child Identity Theft."

9 Schoepfer, "Studying the Correlates of Fraud Victimization and Reporting," p. 211.

10 Yuille, "Child Identity Theft."

11 Friedrichs, *Trusted Criminals*, pp. 50–52.

12 Ibid.

13 Ibid., pp. 50–53; Ellen S. Podgor, "Throwing Away the Key," *Yale Law Journal*. 116: Pocket part 279 (2007). Available online. URL: http://thepocketpart.org/2007/02/21/podgor.html.

14 Ibid.

15 Friedrichs, *Trusted Criminals*, p. 53.

16 Neal Shover, Greer Litton Fox, and Michael Mills, "Long-Term

Consequences of Victimization by White-Collar Crime," *Justice Quarterly* 11:1 (March 1994): pp. 75–76.

Point: White-Collar Penalties Are Too Lenient

1 Carol A. Halbrooks, "It Can Happen Here," *Newsweek*, November 26, 1990, p. 10.

2 Ibid.

3 Ibid.

4 Friedrichs, *Trusted Criminals*, pp. 45–48.

5 Kip Schlegel, "Transnational Crime: Implications for Local Law Enforcement," *Journal of Contemporary Criminal Justice* 16:365 (2000): p. 367.

6 Ibid.

7 Friedrichs, *Trusted Criminals*, pp. 46–48.

8 "Best Places to Go to Prison: Federal Prison Camp Eglin," Forbes.com. September 12, 2002. Available online. URL: http://www.forbes.com/2002/09/12/bestprisonslide_2.html?thisSpeed=30000.

9 "Best Places to Go to Prison: Federal Correctional Institute Morgantown," Forbes.com. September 12, 2002. Available online. URL: http://www.forbes.com/2002/09/12/bestprisonslide_4.html?thisSpeed=30000.

10 "Best Places to Go to Prison: Federal Prison Camp Otisville," Forbes.com. September 12, 2002. Available online. URL: http://www.forbes.com/2002/09/12/bestprisonslide_5.html?thisSpeed=30000.

11 Victor F. Zonana, "Pact Will Allow Milken to Keep $125 Million—Litigation: Imprisoned Financier's Family to Retain Up to $400 Million in Proposed Settlement of 150 Suits," *Los Angeles Times*, February 28, 1992. Available online. URL: http://articles.latimes.com/1992-02-28/news/mn-2955_1_michael-milken.

12 United States Sentencing Commission, *United States Sentencing Commission Guidelines Manual*, 2004, Available online. URL: http://www.ussc.gov/2004guid/gl2004.pdf.

13 Associated Press, "Obama Seeks Crack Cocaine Sentence Changes," MSNBC.com, April 29, 2009, Available online. URL: http://www.msnbc.msn.com/id/30479677.

14 "Cocaine Prices," Crack Cocaine.org, 2008. Available online. URL: http://www.crack-cocaine.org/cocaine-prices.htm.

15 David Shestokas, "The Purpose of Criminal Punishment: Why Impose Penalties on Law Breakers?" Suite101.com, March 10, 2009. Available online. URL: http://peacesecurity.suite101.com/article.cfm/the_purpose_of_criminal_punishment.

16 Kevin McCoy, "Madoff Victims Describe Pain of Fraud to Judge," *USA Today*, June 16, 2009. Available online. URL: http://www.usatoday.com/money/markets/2009-06-15-madoff-victims_N.htm.

17 Ibid.

18 Ibid.

19 J. Scott Dutcher, "From the Boardroom to the Cellblock: The Justifications for Harsher Punishment of White-Collar and Corporate Crime," *Arizona State Law Journal.* 37:1295, 1301 (2005).

20 David Feige, "How to Deter White-Collar Crime," *The Nation*, June 23, 2005. Available online. URL: http://www.thenation.com/doc/20050711/feige.

Counterpoint: White-Collar Penalties Are Appropriately Harsh

1 A Google.com search of "Bernard Madoff" on July 26, 2009 resulted in 9.8 million hits from news, blogs, and other sites.

2 Alison Cies, "Madoff's Victims Speak Out," *Jewish Daily Forward*, June 24, 2009. Available online. URL: http://www.forward.com/articles/108462/.

3 Genevieve Reilly, "Local Madoff Victims Speak Out," *Connecticut Post*, April 10, 2009. Available online. URL: http://www.connpost.com/news/ci_11889394?source=rss.

4 Kevin Johnson, "Prison Coaches Charge Up to $20,000 to Prep White-Collar Perps," USAToday.com, July 14, 2009. Available online. URL: http://www.usatoday.com/news/nation/2009-07-14-prison101_N.htm.

5 Anthony Lin, "Punishing White Collar Crime: Chinese Style," LegalWeek.com, January 16, 2009. Available online. URL: http://www.legalweekblogs.com/legalvillage/2009/01/punishing_white_collar_crime_c.html.

6 Ron Shinkman, "Why Bernard Madoff Should Face the Death Penalty," OpEdNews.com, March 14, 2009. Available online. URL: http://www.opednews.com/articles/Why-Bernard-Madoff-Should-by-Ron-Shinkman-090313-501.html.

7 Hazel Croall, "Victims of White-Collar and Corporate Crime," *Applied Criminology*, Brian Stout, et. al., eds., Thousand Oaks, Calif.: Sage Publications, 2008.

8 Ellen Podgor, "The Challenge of White-Collar Sentencing," *Journal of Criminal Law & Criminology.* 97:731 (2007).

9 Harlan Protass, "Even Bernard Madoff Doesn't Deserve This," *Washington Post*, December 21, 2008, p. B04.

10 Associated Press, "Madoff Sentenced to 150 Years in Prison," MSNBC.com, June 29, 2009.

11 Brian Dakss, "Martha Prison No 'Camp Cupcake,'" CBS News, October 7, 2004. Available online. URL: http://www.cbsnews.com/stories/2004/10/07/earlyshow/main647995.shtml.

12 Shestokas, "The Purpose of Criminal Punishment."

13 Podgor, "Throwing Away the Key."

14 Shinkman, "Why Bernard Madoff Should Face the Death Penalty"; Lin, "Punishing White Collar Crime: Chinese Style."

15 David DuMoucel, George Donnini, Joseph Richotte, "Sentencing Advocacy for White Collar Defendants: Show Some Gall," *WCC Bulletin, American Bar Association*, February 2008. Available online. URL: http://www.abanet.org/crimjust/wcc/feb08dumouchel.htm.

16 "Martha: Prison Food Is Lousy," CNN/Money, December 22, 2004. Available online. URL: http://money.cnn.com/2004/12/22/news/newsmakers/martha/index.htm.

17 Friedrichs, *Trusted Criminals*, p. 293.

Point: Government Must Protect Citizens from White-Collar Crime

1 Robert Draper, "The Toxic Pharmacist," *New York Times*, June 8, 2003. Available online. URL: http://www.nytimes.com/2003/06/08/magazine/the-toxic-pharmacist.html.

2 Ibid.

3 Ibid.

4 Ibid.

5 Lloyd de Vries, "Thousands of Diluted Drug Doses," CBS News, April 19, 2002. Available online. URL: http://www.cbsnews.com/stories/2002/04/19/national/main506777.shtml.

6 Draper, "The Toxic Pharmacist."

7 Kenneth Janda, et. al., *The Challenge of Democracy*, 9th ed., Florence, Ken.: Cengage Publishing, 2006, pp. 2–8.

8 "Oliver Wendell Holmes Quotes," Thinkexist.com. Available online. URL: http://thinkexist.com/

quotation/the_right_to_swing_my_
fist_ends_where_the_other/217369.
html.

9 Dutcher, "From the Boardroom to the
   Cellblock."

10 Marcie Gordon, "Firm Linked to
   Madoff Charged in Scandal," *Deseret
   News*, June 23, 2009. Available online.
   URL: http://findarticles.com/p/
   articles/mi_qn4188/is_20090623/
   ai_n32088951/.

11 George Reisman, *Capitalism*, Ch. 20,
   Ottawa, Ill.: Jameson Books, 1990.

12 Friedrichs, *Trusted Criminals*, p. 49.

13 Office of Management and Budget,
   "2003 Report to Congress on the Costs
   and Benefits of Federal Regulation,"
   Federal Register, vol. 68, num. 22, February 3, 2003.

14 Ibid.

Counterpoint: Government Regulation of White-Collar Crime Is Ineffective

1 "Key Facts," Bristol-Myers Squibb,
   2009. Available online. URL: http://
   www.bms.com/ourcompany/Pages/
   keyfacts.aspx.

2 Lisa Brennan, "Deferred White-Collar
   Prosecutions: New Terrain, Few
   Signposts," *New Jersey Law Journal*,
   April 11, 2006. Available online.
   URL: http://www.law.com/jsp/article.
   jsp?id=1144330167949.

3 Richard Epstein, "The Deferred Prosecution Racket," *Wall Street Journal*,
   November 26, 2006. Available online.
   URL: http://online.wsj.com/article_
   print/SB116468395737834160.html.

4 Brennan, "Deferred White-Collar
   Prosecutions."

5 Epstein, "The Deferred Prosecution
   Racket."

6 Ibid.

7 Brennan, "Deferred White-Collar
   Prosecutions."

8 Ibid.

9 Cristie Ford and David Hess, "Can
   Corporate Monitorships Improve
   Corporate Compliance?" *Journal of
   Corporate Law*. 34:3 (Spring 2009):
   pp. 679.

10 Terry Leap, *Dishonest Dollars*, Ithaca,
   N.Y.: ILR Press, 2007, pp. 164–165.

11 Reisman, *Capitalism*, pp. 985–988.

12 Kurt Eichenwald, "Arthur Andersen
   Is Said to be Near Sale to Rival," *New
   York Times*, March 11, 2002. Available
   online. URL: http://www.nytimes.
   com/2002/03/11/business/arthur-
   andersen-is-said-to-be-near-a-sale-
   to-a-rival.html?pagewanted=2.

13 *Arthur Andersen v. the United States*,
   544 U.S. 696 (2005).

14 Associated Press, "Martha Stewart in
   Court for Appeals Hearing," MSNBC.
   com, March 18, 2005. Available
   online. URL: http://www.msnbc.msn.
   com/id/7219340.

15 Friedrichs, *Trusted Criminals*, p. 257.

16 Richard Epstein, *Overdose: How
   Excessive Government Regulation Stifles Pharmaceutical Innovation*, New
   Haven, Conn.: Yale University Press,
   2006.

17 Brennan, "Deferred."

18 Lynnley Browning, "Charges Dropped
   Against 13 in KPMG Tax Shelter
   Case," *New York Times*, July 17, 2007.
   Available online. URL: http://www.
   nytimes.com/2007/07/17/business/
   kpmg-web.html?_r=2&ref=business&
   oref=slogin.

19 John Carney, "Case Dismissed! Judge
   Kaplan Dismisses Case Against 13
   KPMG Defendants," *Dealbreaker*,
   June 17, 2007. Available online. URL:
   http://dealbreaker.com/kpmg/.

Conclusion: The Future of White-Collar Crime

1 Larry Neumeister and Tom Hays,
   "Madoff Sentenced to 150 Years for
   Massive Fraud Scheme," Associ-
   ated Press, June 29, 2009. Available

online. URL: http://hamptonroads.com/2009/06/madoff-sentenced-150-years-massive-fraud-scheme.

2 Mark Weisbrot, "Analysis: Housing Bubble Burst Sending Economy Down," *Pittsburgh Post Gazette*, January 3, 2007. Available online. URL: http://www.post-gazette.com/pg/07003/750746-28.stm.

3 Bianna Golodryga and Lee Farran, "Failure in Auto Industry Could Affect 13 Million Jobs," ABCNews.com, Nov. 18, 2008. Available online. URL: http://abcnews.go.com/GMA/story?id=6278396&page=1.

4 Terry Leap, *Dishonest Dollars*, p. 196.

5 Ibid., pp. 196–198.

6 Friedrich, *Trusted Criminals*, p. 22.

7 John Hasnas, "Overcriminalization: The Politics of Crime: Ethics and the Problem of White Collar Crime," *American University Law Review.* 54:579 (February 2005).

8 Elizabeth Moore and Michael Mills, "The Neglected Victims and Unexamined Costs of White-Collar Crimes," *Crime and Delinquency.* 36:3 (1990): pp. 408–418, 410.

9 "Welcome to the Office for Victims of Crimes," Department of Justice. Available online. URL: http://www.ojp.usdoj.gov/ovc/welcovc/welcome.html.

10 "Elie Wiesel Says He Can't Forgive Bernie Madoff," CNN.com.

RESOURCES ||||▷

Books and Articles

Associated Press. "Obama Seeks Crack Cocaine Sentence Changes," MSNBC.com, April 29, 2009. Available online. URL: http://www.msnbc.msn.com/id/30479677.

———. "Ex-Financier Madoff Pleads Guilty to All Charges," MSNBC.com, March 12, 2009. Available online. URL: http://www.msnbc.msn.com/id/29651773/.

———. "Madoff Sentenced to 150 Years in Prison," MSNBC.com, June 29, 2009.

Baker, John S., Jr. "The Sociological Origins of 'White Collar Crime,'" *Legal Memorandum #14,* The Heritage Foundation, October 4, 2004. Available online. URL: http://www.heritage.org/research/legalissues/lm14.cfm.

Berlau, John. "Freedom and Its Digital Discontents." *The Economist*, March 17, 2008. Available online. URL: http://cei.org/articles/freedom-and-its-digital-discontents.

"Best Places to Go to Prison: Federal Correctional Institute Morgantown," Forbes.com. September 12, 2002. Available online. URL: http://www.forbes.com/2002/09/12/bestprisonslide_4.html?thisSpeed=30000.

"Best Places to Go to Prison: Federal Prison Camp Eglin," Forbes.com. September 12, 2002. Available online. URL: http://www.forbes.com/2002/09/12/bestprisonslide_2.html?thisSpeed=30000.

"Best Places to Go to Prison: Federal Prison Camp Otisville," Forbes.com. September 12, 2002. Available online. URL: http://www.forbes.com/2002/09/12/bestprisonslide_5.html?thisSpeed=30000.

Biagioli, Antonello. "Financial Crime as a Threat to the Wealth of Nations: A Cost-Effectiveness Approach." *Journal of Money Laundering Control.* 1:11 (2008): pp. 88–95.

Black, Henry Campbell. "Crime," *Black's Law Dictionary*, 7th ed. St. Paul, Minn.: West Publishing, 1999.

Chase, Christopher R. "To Shred or Not to Shred: Document Retention Policies and Federal Obstruction of Justice Statutes." *Fordham Journal of Corporate & Financial Law.* 8:721 (2003): pp. 740–743.

Cies, Alison. "Madoff's Victims Speak Out." *Jewish Daily Forward*, June 24, 2009. Available online. URL: http://www.forward.com/articles/108462/.

"Cocaine Prices," Crack Cocaine.org, 2008. Available online. URL: http://www.crack-cocaine.org/cocaine-prices.htm.

Crews, Clyde Wayne. "Ten Thousand Commandments 2009," Competitive Enterprise Institute, May 28, 2009. Available online. URL: http://cei.org/issue-analysis/2009/05/28/ten-thousand-commandments.

Croall, Hazel. "Victims of White-Collar and Corporate Crime." *Applied Criminology*, Brian Stout, et. al., eds. Thousand Oaks, Calif.: Sage Publications, 2008.

Dakss, Brian. "Martha Prison No 'Camp Cupcake,'" CBSNews.com, October 7, 2004. Available online. URL: http://www.cbsnews.com/stories/2004/10/07/earlyshow/main647995.shtml.

de Vries, Lloyd. "Thousands of Diluted Drug Doses," CBSNews.com, April 19, 2002. Available online. URL: http://www.cbsnews.com/stories/2002/04/19/national/main506777.shtml.

Draper, Robert. "The Toxic Pharmacist." *New York Times*, June 8, 2003. Available online. URL: http://www.nytimes.com/2003/06/08/magazine/the-toxic-pharmacist.html?sec=health&pagewanted=1.

Dutcher, J. Scott. "From the Boardroom to the Cellblock: The Justifications for Harsher Punishment of White-Collar and Corporate Crime." *Arizona State Law Journal*. 37:1295 (2005).

DuMoucel, David, George Donnini, and Joseph Richotte. "Sentencing Advocacy for White Collar Defendants: Show Some Gall." *WCC Bulletin, American Bar Association*, February 2008. Available online. URL: http://www.abanet.org/crimjust/wcc/feb08dumouchel.htm.

"Elie Wiesel Says He Can't Forgive Bernie Madoff," CNN.com, February 27, 2009. Available online. URL: http://www.cnn.com/2009/CRIME/02/27/wiesel.madoff/.

Exodus 20:15-16, *Holy Bible*, New Revised Standard Version.

"Facts and Figures 2003: White Collar Crime," Federal Bureau of Investigation. Available online. URL: http://www.fbi.gov/libref/factsfigure/wcc.htm.

Friedrichs, David O. *Trusted Criminals: White Collar Crime in Contemporary Society*, 3rd ed., Belmont, Calif.: Thomson/Wadsworth, 2007.

Geis, Gilbert. *White-Collar and Corporate Crime.* Upper Saddle River, N.J.: Pearson Education, 2007.

Golodryga, Bianna, and Lee Farran. "Failure in Auto Industry Could Affect 13 Million Jobs," ABCNews.com, November 18, 2008. Available online. URL: http://abcnews.go.com/GMA/story?id=6278396&page=1.

Gordon, Marcie. "Firm Linked to Madoff Charged in Scandal." *Deseret News*, June 23, 2009. Available online. URL: http://findarticles.com/p/articles/mi_qn4188/is_20090623/ai_n32088951/.

Green, Stuart. "The Concept of White Collar Crime in Law and Legal Theory." *Buffalo Criminal Law Review.* 8:1 (2005).

Grundfest, Joseph A. and Steven E. Bochner. "Fixing 404." *Michigan Law Review.* 105:1643 (2007).

Halbrooks, Carol A. "It Can Happen Here." *Newsweek*, November 26, 1990, p. 10.

Hasnas, John. "Overcriminalization: The Politics of Crime: Ethics and the Problem of White Collar Crime." *American University Law Review.* 579 (February 2005).

Janda, Kenneth, et. al. *The Challenge of Democracy*, 9th ed. Florence, Ken.: Cengage Publishing, 2006.

Johnson, Kevin. "Prison Coaches Charge Up to $20,000 to Prep White-Collar Perps." *USAToday*, July 14, 2009. Available online. URL: http://www.usatoday.com/news/nation/2009-07-14-prison101_N.htm.

Knight, Alfred H. *The Life of the Law.* New York: Crown Publishers, 1996.

Leap, Terry. *Dishonest Dollars.* Ithaca, N.Y.: Cornell University Press, 2007.

Lin, Anthony. "Punishing White Collar Crime: Chinese Style," LegalWeek.com. January 16, 2009. Available online. URL: http://www.legalweekblogs.com/legalvillage/2009/01/punishing_white_collar_crime_c.html.

Lucas, Nance. "An Interview with United States Senator Paul S. Sarbanes." *Journal of Leadership & Organizational Studies*, Summer 2004. Available

online. URL: http://findarticles.com/p/articles/mi_m0NXD/is_1_11/ai_
n25101748/?tag=content;col1.

"Madoff Investor Found Dead in Apparent Suicide," CNN.com, December 24, 2008. Available online. URL: http://www.cnn.com/2008/
CRIME/12/23/madoff.investor.suicide/index.html.

"Madoff's Victims." *Wall Street Journal*, February 5, 2009. Available online.
URL: http://s.wsj.net/public/resources/documents/st_madoff_victims_
20081215.html.

Marshall, Gordon. "Crime," *A Dictionary of Sociology*, 1998. Encyclopedia.
com, May 13, 2009. Available online. URL: http://www.encyclopedia.com.

"Martha: Prison Food Is Lousy." CNN/Money, December 22, 2004. Available online. URL: http://money.cnn.com/2004/12/22/news/newsmakers/
martha/index.htm.

McCoy, Kevin. "Madoff Victims Describe Pain of Fraud to Judge." *USA
Today*, June 16, 2009. Available online. URL: http://www.usatoday.com/
money/markets/2009-06-15-madoff-victims_N.htm.

Moore, Elizabeth, and Michael Mills. "The Neglected Victims and Unexamined Costs of White-Collar Crimes." *Crime and Delinquency*. 36:3 (1990):
pp. 408–418.

Neumeister, Larry, and Tom Hays. "Madoff Sentenced to 150 Years for Massive Fraud Scheme," Associated Press, June 29, 2009. Available online.
URL: http://hamptonroads.com/2009/06/madoff-sentenced-150-years-
massive-fraud-scheme.

NPR Radio. "From Milken to Madoff: White-Collar Crime in Focus," NPR.
org, January 8, 2009. Available online. URL: http://www.npr.org/
templates/story/story.php?storyId=99120924.

Office of Management and Budget. "2003 Report to Congress on the Costs
and Benefits of Federal Regulation." *Federal Register*. 68:22 (February 3,
2003).

"Oliver Wendell Holmes Quotes," Thinkexist.com. Available online. URL:
http://thinkexist.com/quotation/the_right_to_swing_my_fist_ends_
where_the_other/217369.html.

Podgor, Ellen S. "The Challenge of White-Collar Sentencing." *Journal of Criminal Law & Criminology*. 97:731 (2007).

———. "Throwing Away the Key," *Yale Law Journal* 116: Pocket Part 279, 284, 2007. Available online. URL: http://thepocketpart.org/2007/02/21/podgor.html.

———. "White-Collar Crime: A Letter from the Future." *Ohio State Journal of Criminal Law*. 5 (2007): p. 247.

Pontell, Henry N. "White Collar Crime and Major Financial Debacles in the United States." *Resource Materials Series*, no. 67, United Nations Asia and Far East Institute for the Prevention of Crime and Treatment of Offenders, December 2005. Available online. URL: http://www.unafei.or.jp/english/pdf/PDF_rms/no67/15_Pontell_p189-p201.pdf.

Protass, Harlan. "Even Bernard Madoff Doesn't Deserve This." *Washington Post*, Dec. 21, 2008, p. B04.

Quran, 61:2–3.

Recine, Jennifer S. "Examination of the White Collar Crime Penalty Enhancements in the Sarbanes-Oxley Act." *American Criminal Law Review*. 39:1535 (Fall 2002).

Reilly, Genevieve. "Local Madoff Victims Speak Out." *Connecticut Post*, April 10, 2009. Available online. URL: http://www.connpost.com/news/ci_11889394?source=rss.

Roberts, Johnnie. "Do the Media Hate the Rich?" *Newsweek*, June 12, 2009. Available online. URL: http://www.newsweek.com/id/201864.

Schlegel, Kip. "Transnational Crime: Implications for Local Law Enforcement." *Journal of Contemporary Criminal Justice*. 16:365 (2000).

Schoepfer, Andrea, and Nicole Leeper Piquero. "Studying the Correlates of Fraud Victimization and Reporting." *Journal of Criminal Justice*. 37 (2009).

Shestokas, David. "The Purpose of Criminal Punishment: Why Impose Penalties on Law Breakers?" Suite101.com, March 10, 2009. Available online. URL: http://peacesecurity.suite101.com/article.cfm/the_purpose_of_criminal_punishment.

Shinkman, Ron. "Why Bernard Madoff Should Face the Death Penalty." OpEdNews.com, March 14, 2009. Available online. URL: http://www. opednews.com/articles/Why-Bernard-Madoff-Should-by-Ron-Shinkman-090313-501.html.

Shover, Neal, Greer Litton Fox, and Michael Mills. "Long-Term Consequences of Victimization by White-Collar Crime." *Justice Quarterly*. 11:1 (March 1994).

Spalding, Albert D., Jr., and Mary Ashbey Morrison. "Criminal Liability for Document Shredding after Arthur Andersen, LLP." *American Business Law Journal*. 43:647 (2006).

Sutherland, Edwin H. *White Collar Crime: The Uncut Version*. New Haven, Conn.: Yale University Press, 1983.

"The Story of Bronti Kelly," MyIDfix.com. Available online. URL: http://www.myidfix.com/identity-theft-stories.php.

18 United States Code 1512(c).

United States Sentencing Commission. United States Sentencing Commission Guidelines Manual, 2004. Available online. URL: http://www.ussc.gov/2004guid/gl2004.pdf.

Weisbrot, Mark. "Analysis: Housing Bubble Burst Sending Economy Down." *Pittsburgh Post Gazette*, January 3, 2007. Available online. URL: http://www.post-gazette.com/pg/07003/750746-28.stm.

"Welcome to the Office for Victims of Crimes," Department of Justice. Available online. URL: http://www.ojp.usdoj.gov/ovc/welcovc/welcome.html.

Williams, Rachel. "Madoff Fraud Victim Killed Himself to Avoid Bankruptcy." *Guardian*, June 11, 2009. Available online. URL: http://www.guardian.co.uk/uk/2009/jun/11/madoff-victim-suicide.

Yuille, Brigitte. "Child Identity Theft: A Victim's Story," Bankrate.com, January 3, 2007. Available online. URL: http://www.bankrate.com/brm/news/debt/20070103_child_identity_theft_f1.asp.

Zakaria, Fareed. "A Capitalist Manifesto: Greed Is Good (To a Point)." *Newsweek*, June 13, 2009. Available online. URL: http://www.newsweek.com/id/201935.

Zonana, Victor F. "Pact Will Allow Milken to Keep $125 Million—Litigation: Imprisoned Financier's Family to Retain up to $400 Million in Proposed Settlement of 150 Suits." *Los Angeles Times*, Feb. 28, 2002. Available online. URL: http://articles.latimes.com/1992-02-28/news/mn-2955_1_michael-milken.

Web Sites

Federal Bureau of Investigation–White-Collar Crime
http://www.fbi.gov/whitecollarcrime.htm
> The "White-Collar Crime" page on the FBI Web site includes useful tools and resources for understanding white-collar crime, as well as tips on how to avoid becoming a victim. This site also provides frequently updated white-collar criminal cases.

The Heritage Foundation
http://www.heritage.org
> The Heritage Foundation is a conservative think tank with the following mission: "To formulate and promote conservative public policies based on the principles of free enterprise, limited government, individual freedom, traditional American values, and a strong national defense." This site provides research packets, information on conferences, and news feeds related to white-collar crime.

Legal Information Institute
http://www.law.cornell.edu/
> "The Legal Information Institute (LII) is a research and electronic publishing activity of the Cornell Law School. Popular collections include the U.S. Code and Supreme Court opinions." This site is particularly useful as a research tool when looking for statutes and court cases.

National White Collar Crime Center
http://www.NW3C.org
> The National White Collar Crime Center is an organization dedicated to providing national and international support for preventing and prosecuting white-collar crimes. "The mission of the National White Collar Crime Center (NW3C) is to provide training, investigative support and research to agencies and entities involved in the prevention, investigation and prosecution of economic and high-tech crime." This site is useful for finding research and practical assistance when dealing with white-collar crime.

Securities and Exchange Commission

http://www.SEC.gov

"The mission of the U.S. Securities and Exchange Commission is to protect investors; maintain fair, orderly, and efficient markets; and facilitate capital formation." As part of that mission, the SEC uses this Web site to provide resources for all people involved or interested in financial markets. This site provides impressive amounts of information on the specifics of how markets work and are regulated.

PICTURE CREDITS

JOHN E. FERGUSON JR. is a lecturer at the Hankamer School of Business and in the political science department at Baylor University in Waco, Texas. He earned his M.T.S. and J.D. degrees from Vanderbilt University's Divinity and Law Schools. He has been a member of the bar in Tennessee, Washington, D.C., and the United States Supreme Court.

ALAN MARZILLI, M.A., J.D., lives in Birmingham, Ala., and is a program associate with Advocates for Human Potential, Inc., a research and consulting firm based in Sudbury, Mass., and Albany, N.Y. He primarily works on developing training and educational materials for agencies of the federal government on topics such as housing, mental health policy, employment, and transportation. He has spoken on mental health issues in 30 states, the District of Columbia, and Puerto Rico; his work has included training mental health administrators, nonprofit management and staff, and people with mental illnesses and their families on a wide variety of topics, including effective advocacy, community-based mental health services, and housing. He has written several handbooks and training curricula that are used nationally—as far away as the territory of Guam. He managed statewide and national mental health advocacy programs and worked for several public interest lobbying organizations while studying law at Georgetown University. He has written more than a dozen books, including numerous titles in the POINT/COUNTERPOINT series.